D0636273

P. G. WODEHOUSE
'In His Own Words'

P. G. WODEHOUSE
'In His Own Words'

Barry Day and Tony Ring

HUTCHINSON
London

Extracts from the works of P. G. Wodehouse
© The Trustees of the P. G. Wodehouse Estate 2001

Format and linking narrative copyright © Barry Day 2001

The right of Barry Day and Tony Ring to be identified as the authors
of this work has been asserted by them in accordance with
the Copyright, Designs and Patents Act 1988

First published in the United Kingdom in 2001 by Hutchinson

The Random House Group Limited
20 Vauxhall Bridge Road, London SW1V 2SA

Random House Australia (Pty) Limited
20 Alfred Street, Milsons Point, Sydney,
New South Wales 2061, Australia

Random House New Zealand Limited
18 Poland Road, Glenfield, Auckland 10, New Zealand

Random House (Pty) Limited
Endulini, 5a Jubilee Road, Parktown 2193, South Africa

The Random House Group Limited Reg. No. 954009
www.randomhouse.co.uk

A CIP record for this book is available from the British Library

Papers used by Random House UK Limited are natural,
recyclable products made from wood grown in sustainable forests.
The manufacturing processes conform to the environmental
regulations of the country of origin.

ISBN 0 09 179399 8

Typeset in Perpetua by MATS, Southend-on-Sea, Essex
Printed and bound in Great Britain by
Biddles Ltd, Guildford and King's Lynn

CONTENTS

in his own words...

DEDICATION

In view of the subject's strongly expressed aversion to footnotes ('obscene little fly-specks scattered about all over the page') there will be none in this book. (1) If the attributions given are insufficient for the reader, then, as Wodehouse so eloquently put it elsewhere – 'Sucks to you!'

Nor will there be a Dedication. On the whole he felt its day was probably over. Having in his long career passed through 'the curt, take-it-or-leave-it dedication' – 'To J. Smith' – the 'somewhat warmer' – 'To My Friend Percy Brown' – quite a few of 'those cryptic things with a bit of poetry in italics' –

To F. B. O.

Stark winds
And sunset over the moors
Why?
Whither?
Whence?
And the role of distant drums

– and the occasional 'nasty dedication, intended to sting' –

To J. Alastair Frisby
Who
Told Me I Would Never Have A Book Published
And

Advised Me
To
Get A Job Selling Jellied Eels

— he found himself pondering the questions that had crept into many another author's mind — 'What is there in this for me?' 'What is Wodehouse getting out of this?' I asked myself, and the answer, as far as I could see, was, 'Not a thing.'

Thus, no Dedication (2) ...

(1) From the Foreword to *Over Seventy*.
(2) Except, possibly, 'To Wodehouse, Sir Pelham Grenville, LLD (1881–1975)'.

INTRODUCTION

Watching Alec Guinness over the years gave me pleasure on two distinct levels. There was the consummate actor becoming someone else in front of my eyes and, being interviewed, there was the private man, modest and reclusive, the face a blank page on which any character could be drawn.

Except . . . why did I find myself wondering whether this wasn't simply one more performance and perhaps one of his most effective, since to project blandness in an age geared to glamour and excitement guaranteed him a degree of the privacy he clearly craved. In other words – how do we know when an actor isn't *acting*?

Something comparable happens when you come to deal with Wodehouse and his life, though in his case it takes place on three parallel planes. There are the bare bones of factual data, occasionally augmented by his own diary notes; there are his 'autobiographical' writings and letters (of which more anon); and there are the transpositions from the factual to the fictional world of the novels and stories. And somewhere in that narrative curve lies a version of the way things were with this remarkable storyteller. In other words – how do we know when a storyteller isn't telling a *story*?

Wodehouse himself gives us a warning clue in his 1946 correspondence with Guy Bolton prior to the writing of *Bring On the Girls,* their collaborative account of their years in the musical theatre . . .

I think we shall have to let truth go to the wall
if it interferes with entertainment . . . That is

what we want to avoid in this book — shoving
in stuff just because it happened. Even if we
have to invent every line of the thing, we
must have entertainment.

When it came to the collection of his letters to his old friend,
William Townend — published as *Performing Flea* (UK, 1953)
and *Author! Author!* (US, substantially revised, 1962) — the same
thought process was clearly at work. Writing to Townend in
response to his original suggestion, Wodehouse makes it clear
that 'the great thing, as I see it, is not to feel ourselves confined
to the actual letters. I mean, nobody knows what was actually in
the letters, so we can fake as much as we like . . . Also, these
letters give me a wonderful opportunity of shoving in thoughts
on life to a much greater extent than I do in my actual letters
. . . I have always wanted to write my autobiography but felt
too self-conscious. This will be a way of doing the thing
obliquely.'

For a man who — like Alec Guinness — professed to be
nothing more than a simple, retiring sort of chap, never so
happy (in Wodehouse's case) as when he was peacefully pecking
away at his old manual typewriter, these occasional insights
pose a fascinating possibility . . .

Was the 'Plum' Wodehouse we thought we knew — the
pipe-smoking, Peke-loving chap exclusively inhabiting some
private and personal universe he carried around in his head —
perhaps his own finest creation? Was this divine dottiness, this
amiable otherworldliness the perfect protection used by a man
shrewd enough in the ways of the world to realise that it was the
perfect way to ensure the privacy he craved to do the one thing
he was driven to do — write?

In the same letter to Bolton he tells his friend firmly that he will have to fill in the local contemporary colour, because 'I am so constituted as to never notice what is going on around me and, if asked, would say that there have been no changes in New York since 1916.' Isn't there a note here of protesting a little *too* much?

'So, how do we know that Mr Wodehouse is an unworldly literary recluse, Watson? Elementary. Mr Wodehouse makes sure to constantly tell us so himself.'

Which raises another speculation . . . Who was it who said: 'They became what they beheld'? Does constant repetition of a single part eventually turn the actor into the character he is portraying?

Holmes would probably go on to prove with ample textual reference that Wodehouse merely found the temporal trappings uninteresting and irrelevant to the imaginative world he wished to celebrate. Certainly, he missed none of the behavioural clues to the *comédie humaine* that went on all around him. However stylised his characters may be, their *characteristics* are universal. If we did not see ourselves in their foibles and failings, we shouldn't find them amusing, since the basis of all comedy is truth.

If I compare Wodehouse to Oscar Wilde, I can already sense a *frisson* among Wodehouseans. Yet there are important similarities. In the last hundred years or so, no one – with the possible exception of Noël Coward – has used words with such consistent wit. (Both Coward and Wilde, incidentally, used their work to create and maintain their desired persona.) And no one has so clearly perceived their own lives as a continuing work of fiction.

Wilde came to see his life as a play – in his case, one that didn't follow the plot he had envisaged. Nonetheless, he was determined to act it out, rather than bring down the curtain.

Wodehouse lived in the imaginative universe of humorous fantasy he had pieced together from the elements of his own early Edwardian life that had pleased him most, ignoring those that did not. Although best known for his fiction, the Wodehouse world owes its distinctive structure to the musical comedies of his early years. He himself referred to his early novels as 'musical comedies without the music' and thought of them in terms of 'acts, chorus numbers, duets and solos'. The experience taught him that the only way to write a story was 'to split it up into scenes and have as little stuff between the scenes as possible.'

And, by definition, what was good enough for telling a story was surely good enough when it came to telling the story of your own life.

In any case, where was the boundary between the one and the other? So, with that small *caveat lector*, let us begin . . .

BARRY DAY
2001

A NOTE ON SOURCES

Wodehouse's words are drawn from his three 'auto-biographical' works — *Over Seventy* (*America, I Like You* in US), *Performing Flea* (*Author! Author!* in US), *Bring on the Girls,* his letters, miscellaneous interviews and, of course, the fiction. In almost all cases the quotations are attributed but in the case of some of the interview material — where Wodehouse was inclined to repeat (and occasionally contradict himself) on minor points, we have taken the liberty of condensing it for easier reading. In those cases you will have to take our word for it that all the words are vintage Wodehouse.

Song lyrics are reproduced by kind permission of Warner Chappell and Universal Music Publications Ltd.

Lines from ''S Wonderful' are used by kind permission of the Ira Gershwin Estate.

The typewriter illustration is reproduced by kind permission of Lynne Carey.

Illustrations by Geoffrey Salter are reproduced by kind permission of Penguin Books.

Lyrics from 'Greenwich Village' (Kern/Wodehouse) © 1918 by kind permission of Universal Music Publishing Ltd.

Lyrics from 'Bongo On The Congo' (Kern/Wodehouse) © 1924 by kind permission of Universal Music Publishing Ltd.

Lyrics from 'All You Need Is A Girl' (Kern/Wodehouse) © 1924 by kind permission of Universal Music Publishing Ltd.

Lyrics from 'The Little Church Around The Corner' (Kern/Wodehouse) © 1907 by kind permission of Universal Music Publishing Ltd.

Lyrics from 'You Never Knew About Me' (Kern/Wodehouse) © 1917 by kind permission of Universal Music Publishing Ltd.

CHAPTER ONE

Young Plum

*

'Do you really want to hear the story of my life,
Biscuit?' he said wistfully. 'Sure it won't bore you?'
'Bore me? My dear chap! I'm agog. Let's have the
whole thing. Start from the beginning. Childhood –
early surroundings – genius probably inherited
from male grand-parent – push along.'

    (*Big Money*)

P. G. Wodehouse was born at 1 Vale Place, Epsom Road, Guildford, Surrey on 15 October 1881, the third son of Ernest and Eleanor Wodehouse.

If you ask me to tell you frankly if I like the names Pelham Grenville, I must confess that I do not. I have my dark moods when they seem to me about as low as you can get . . . At the font I remember protesting vigorously when the clergyman uttered them, but he stuck to his point. 'Be that as it may,' he said firmly, having waited for a lull, 'I name thee Pelham Grenville' . . . I was named after a godfather, and not a thing to show for it but a small silver mug which I lost in 1897 . . . I little knew how the frightful label was going to pay off thirty-four years later. (One could do a bit of moralising about that if one wanted to, but better not for the moment. Some other time, perhaps.) . . .

(Preface to Something Fresh)

In his formative years the young Wodehouse understandably had trouble pronouncing a mouthful like 'Pelham'. It tended to come out as 'Plum' and the affectionate diminutive stuck with him for life.

The Wodehouses could, had they chosen to, have laid claim to a rather distinguished family tree. Some reference books trace the lineage back to the Norman Conquest and Lady Mary Boleyn – sister to Anne – certainly crops up there. Although he made little overt mention of it, there is evidence that he was quietly proud of his origins.

In *Thank You, Jeeves* he has Bertie say:

> I think that in about another half jiffy I should have been snorting, if not actually shouting, the ancient battle cry of the Woosters . . . There comes a moment when a fellow must remember that his ancestors did dashed well at the Battle of Crécy and put the old foot down.

And should he ever forget, he has his Aunt Dahlia to remind him:

> Where's your pride, Bertie? Have you forgotten your illustrious ancestors? There was a Wooster at the time of the Crusades who would have won the Battle of Joppa single-handed, if he hadn't fallen off his horse.'
>
> *(Aunts Aren't Gentlemen)*

To judge by the portraits of him as a child, there is every likelihood that Wodehouse was a bonny baby himself but babies *sui generis* tend to fare poorly in the Wodehouse canon. One might well speculate that he shared the well-defined views of his hero Freddie Widgeon in 'Noblesse Oblige' from *Young Men in Spats:*

> It would be paltering with the truth to say that he likes babies. They give him, he says, a sort of grey feeling. He resents their cold stare and the supercilious and up-stage way in which they dribble out of the corner of their mouths on seeing him. Eyeing them he is conscious of doubts as to whether Man can really be Nature's last word.

> Observing what it was that Bingo was carrying, Oofy backed hastily.
> 'Hey!' he exclaimed. 'Don't point that thing at me!'
> 'It's only my baby.'
> 'I dare say. But point it the other way.'
> ('Leave It to Algy' – *A Few Quick Ones*)

In *Eggs, Beans and Crumpets* a baby is described as being 'blob-faced' but then

> 'There's never been much difference between babies of that age. They all look like Winston Churchill.'
> (Cortin in the unproduced play *Arthur*)

[4]

Another baby looked like 'a homicidal fried egg', and when it smiled, 'a slit appeared in the baby's face'.

Nor, according to Wodehouse, do they improve with keeping:

The infant was looking more than ever like some mass-assassin who has been blackballed by the Devil's Island Social and Outing Club as unfit to associate with the members.

('Sonny Boy' from *Eggs, Beans and Crumpets*)

A spectacled child with a mouth that hung open like a letter-box.

(*The Luck of the Bodkins*)

A small boy with a face like a prune run over by a motor bus.

(*Galahad at Blandings*)

The boy's face closely resembled a ripe tomato with a nose stuck on it.

('The Bishop's Move' from *Meet Mr Mulliner*)

He . . . had the peculiarly loathsome expression which a snub nose sometimes gives to the young.

(*Psmith in the City*)

Wodehouse, of course, was never to have a child of his own, though he eventually acquired a step-daughter who distinctly brightened his days. A. A. Milne later claimed that Wodehouse had once told him that he would quite like a son but 'he would have to be born at the age of fifteen, when he was just getting into the house eleven'.

Wodehouse himself had no recollection of having made such a remark but he did recall having attributed the sentiment to Mike in *Psmith in the City* (1910):

Small boys . . . filled him with a sort of frozen horror. It was his view that a boy should not be exhibited publicly until he had reached an age when he might be in the running for some sort of colours at a public school.

('Odd chap, Milne.')

* * * *

Wodehouse Senior was a magistrate in Hong Kong. Wodehouse Junior describes him as being 'as normal as rice pudding'. Of his mother, significantly, he has nothing to say. To him she was in every way a distant relation — some six thousand miles distant, to be precise. She had given birth to Pelham Grenville at Guildford, Surrey, when on home leave visiting a sister — an early Aunt.

I am told that I was taken to Hong Kong at the age of one, but that was my only visit . . . I

think I started my life in England at the age of
two or three . . .

In fact, he followed the classic pattern of families with 'colonial'
parents, who invariably gave the child over to the care of an
amah or mother substitute when abroad and then returned it to
the old country to be educated. Wodehouse rarely saw his
mother from the age of two until he was well into his teens.
'We looked upon mother more like an aunt,' he recalled. 'She
came home very infrequently.'

My father was very indulgent to us boys, my
mother less so. Having seen practically
nothing of her until I was fifteen, I met her as
virtually a stranger and it was not easy to
establish a cordial relationship. With my
father, on the other hand, I was always on
very good terms – though never in any sense
very close. In those days, parents tended to
live a life apart from their children.

The Wodehouse brothers were entrusted to a governess, Miss
Roper, until P.G. was five, then for the next three years to a
'dame school' run on strict Christian lines by the Misses Florrie
and Cissie Prince:

While my parents were in Hong Kong, my
brothers and I lived with some people called

Prince in South Croydon, and I remember what a rustic place it was then. I once got into trouble for stealing turnips out of a near-by turnip field. It was looked on as a major crime. Probably that is what has given me the respect for the law which I have always had . . . I suppose it was a good bringing up, but it certainly did not tend to make one adventurous. I can't remember having done any other naughty thing the whole of the three years I was there.

'The great event of the year' for him was the visit to Grandmother Wodehouse's:

We were left very much to ourselves . . . Once a day we were taken in to see our grandmother – a wizened old lady who looked just like a monkey and gave us a kindly audience for about ten minutes. Incidentally, I have always felt how lucky I was not to have been born earlier, as I missed the period during which parents beat their sons unmercifully. My father told me that when he was a boy this kindly grandmother used to whale the tar out of him.

He was then sent to Elizabeth College, a small public school in Guernsey, for two years ('the best place for a weak chest was supposed to be the Channel Islands . . .'). He found Guernsey in those days 'a delightful place full of lovely bays and as far as I can remember, our movements were never restricted and we were allowed to roam where we liked. My recollections are all of wandering about the island and of the awful steamer trips back to England. Paddle wheel steamers, like on the Mississippi – very small and rolling with every wave.'

Later he went to a preparatory school at Kearsney in Kent which prepared boys for the Royal Naval College, Dartmouth. Presumably it shared the qualities of all preparatory schools:

> [It] was faintly scented with a composite aroma consisting of roast beef, ink, chalk, and that curious classroom smell which is like nothing else on earth.
>
> (*The Little Nugget*)

It was an unsettled existence, to say the least:

> My parents were in Hong Kong most of the time when I was in the knickerbocker stage, and during my school holidays I was passed from aunt to aunt . . . Looking back I can see that I was just passed from hand to hand . . . I never knew any of them at all . . . It was an odd life with no home to go to, but I have always accepted everything that happens to

me in a philosophical spirit; and I can't remember ever having been unhappy in those days. My feeling now is that it was very decent of those aunts to put up three small boys for all those years. The only thing you could say for us is that we never gave any trouble . . . I had a very happy childhood.

Wodehouse then managed to persuade his father to send him to Dulwich College, where a scholarship of £20 a year certainly helped with the fees. His brother Armine was already there and Wodehouse himself had fallen in love with the place at first sight. Realising that his son's poor eyesight would inevitably put the navy out of reach, Ernest Wodehouse agreed and in 1894 the boy became a boarder.

* * * *

In 1896 Wodehouse's parents returned to England on Ernest's retirement — a retirement caused in a manner worthy of his son's subsequent invention. On a bet he walked around the perimeter of Hong Kong Island in the blazing sun and ended up with severe sunstroke. Whether or not he won the bet is not clear but he did manage to live cheerfully, if precariously, on a pension for the next thirty years. Unfortunately for all concerned, it was paid to him in rupees. ('The rupee is the last thing in the world . . . with which anyone who valued his peace of mind would wish to be associated. It never stayed put for a second. "Watch that rupee!" was the cry in the Wodehouse family.')

To begin with the Wodehouses took a house in Dulwich but soon moved to Shropshire. It was there that Wodehouse developed one of the most meaningful emotional relationships he was ever to know – he acquired a dog, a mongrel named Bob.

In his more settled later life he was rarely to be seen without a dog and usually several. The dog of choice was almost always a Pekinese:

Pekes really are a different race and class. They may try to be democratic, but they don't really accept other dogs as their social equals.

(Letter to William Townend – 15 October 1934)

It looked something like a pen-wiper and something like a piece of hearth-rug. A second and keener inspection revealed it as a Pekinese puppy.

('Goodbye to All Cats' from *Young Men in Spats*)

The Peke sniffed at [the piece of cake] disparagingly, and resumed its steady gaze. It wanted chicken. It is the simple creed of the Peke that, where two human beings are gathered together to eat, chicken must enter the proceedings somewhere.

(*Big Money*)

'Well,' she said, choking on the word like a Pekinese on a chump chop too large for its frail strength.

(*Jeeves and the Feudal Spirit*)

He swallowed convulsively, like a Pekinese taking a pill.

(*The Code of the Woosters*)

The Pekinese dog was hurling abuse in Chinese.

('Birth of a Salesman' from *Nothing Serious*)

The Peke followed him. It appeared to have no legs, but to move by faith alone.

('Lord Emsworth Acts for the Best' from *Blandings Castle*)

In Wodehouse the average dog is likely to receive a more sympathetic review than its average two-legged friend:

''As that dog 'ad 'er breakfast?'
'She was eating a shoe when I saw her last.'
'Ah, well, maybe that'll do her till dinner-time.'

(*Sam the Sudden*)

*

'It's about those dogs of yours. What do they live on?'

'The chairs most of the time.'

(*Full Moon*)

*

Sammy [the bulldog] is the most amiable soul in the world and can be happy with anyone. This is the dog I was given by one of the girls (in *Miss 1917*) and he cost a fortune when we first had him, because he was always liking the looks of passers-by outside our garden gate and trotting out and following them. The first time he disappeared, we gave the man who brought him back ten dollars, and this got around among the local children, and stirred up their business instincts. They would come to our gate and call, 'Sammy, Sammy, Sammy', and out old Sam would waddle, and then they would bring him back with a cheery 'We found your dog wandering down the road, mister' and cash in. I may add that the bottom dropped out of the market and today any child that collects twenty-five cents thinks he has done well.

(Letter to William Townend, 28 February 1920)

There were a few notable exceptions in the canon, however — Bartholomew, the Aberdeen Terrier, being one:

[It] gave me an unpleasant look and said something under its breath in Gaelic.

(*The Code of the Woosters*)

Aberdeen terriers, possibly owing to their heavy eyebrows, always seem to look at you as if they were in the pulpit of some particularly strict Scottish sect and you were a parishioner of dubious reputation sitting in the front row of the stalls.

(*Stiff Upper Lip, Jeeves*)

[Bartholomew] hopped from the bed and, advancing into the middle of the room, took a seat, breathing through the nose with a curious whistling sound, and looking at us from under his eyebrows like a Scottish elder rebuking sin from the pulpit.

(*The Code of the Woosters*)

The dog Bartholomew gave me an un-
pleasantly superior look, as if asking if I were
saved.
(*Stiff Upper Lip, Jeeves*)

It would seem that a dog has to be small to be
fond of a joke. You never find an Irish wolf-
hound trying to be a stand-up comic.
(Introduction to Elliott Erwitt's *Son of Bitch*)

Apart from the gift of tongues, any dog lover is likely to take an
anthropomorphic view, even of the most 'hairy and
nondescript' of the species:

. . . its gaze was cold, wary and suspicious,
like that of a stockbroker who thinks
someone is going to play the confidence trick
on him.
('Lord Emsworth and the Girl Friend' from *Blandings
Castle*)

When he retired — as it turned out — to Remsenburg, Long
Island, after the war, Wodehouse also managed to acquire
assorted cats. In fact, he tended to collect a miscellany of pets
by a combination of accident and design, rather like the way a
magnet collects iron filings. But somehow there was never quite
the same affection, at least in his description of them.

The cat had that air of portly well-being which we associate with those who dwell in cathedral closes . . . for all its sleek exterior [he] was mean and bitter. He had no music in his soul, and was fit for treasons, stratagems and spoils. One could picture him stealing milk from a sick tabby.

('Cats Will Be Cats' from *Mulliner Nights*)

*

'What I've got against cats,' said a Lemon Sour . . . 'is their unreliability. They lack candour and are not square shooters. You get your cat and you call him Thomas or George, as the case may be. So far, so good. Then one morning you wake up and find six kittens in the hat-box and you have to reopen the whole matter, approaching it from an entirely different angle.'

('The Story of Webster' from *Mulliner Nights*)

Webster, of course, was the King of Wodehouse Cats:

Webster was not a natty spectacle. Some tough cats from the public-house on the corner had recently been trying to muscle in on his personal dustbin, and, though he had fought them off, the affair had left its mark upon him. A further section had been removed from his already abbreviated ear, and his once sleek flanks were short of several patches of hair. He looked like the late Legs Diamond after a social evening with a few old friends.

('Cats Will Be Cats' from *Mulliner Nights*)

*

Cats, as a class, have never completely got over the snootiness caused by the fact that in Ancient Egypt they were worshipped as gods.

('The Story of Webster' from *Mulliner Nights*)

Even so, as far as Wodehouse was concerned, if it barked, meowed or chirruped, he was its abject slave. Late in life he and his wife Ethel subsidised the Bide-A-Wee animal shelter.

He was a rather sentimental man, who subscribed to homes for unwanted dogs and cats and rarely failed to cry when watching a motion picture with a sad ending.

(*Do Butlers Burgle Banks?*)

Bertie might complain about his Aunt Agatha because she lavished on the dog McIntosh 'a love which might have been better bestowed on a nephew', but any dog lover – particularly one with a nephew – knows that it was Wodehouse and Aunt Agatha who had the canine/human ratio right.

> Today it is raining again, and your words about 'A wet dog is the lovingest' are ringing in my ears. We have two wet dogs brimming over with lovingness. I can cope with the boxer, who stays put, but the dachshund's heart breaks if I don't have him on my lap. The only way of beating the game is to go about in a bathrobe.
>
> (Letter to Ogden Nash – 13 January 1962)

* * * *

Although he was remorseless in his fiction on the subject of child prodigies, Wodehouse could be said to have been one himself. In a 1965 TV interview he told his friend, Malcolm Muggeridge:

> They tell me I was writing when I was five, but it seems rather extraordinary, doesn't it?

. . . and in a letter to Richard Usborne a decade earlier:

> When I was six years old, I read the whole of Pope's *Iliad*. I can't have been more than six, because I read it at my grandmother's in Worcestershire and she died when I was either six or seven and the house was sold. So it must have been when I was either six or seven, and I remember loving it.

But while he may have been a literary lion in embryo, he recalled that his social skills were not nearly as well developed:

> Even at the age of ten I was a social bust, contributing little or nothing to the feast of reason or the flow of soul beyond shuffling my feet and kicking the leg of the chair into which loving hands had dumped me.

In short:

> Boyhood, like measles, is one of those complaints which a man should catch young and have done with.
>
> (*Uneasy Money*)

CHAPTER TWO

Upstairs . . .
Amitae, Materterae* . . .
And Other Relations

It's no use telling me that there are bad aunts and good aunts. At the core they are all alike. Sooner or later, out pops the cloven hoof.

(*The Code of the Woosters*)

In this life it is not aunts that matter but the courage which one brings to them.

(*The Mating Season*)

*Paternal and maternal aunts.
(*Sorry about the footnote!*)

We would spend our holidays with various aunts, some of whom I liked but one or two of whom were very formidable Victorian women.

* * * *

In the Wodehouse vocabulary — indeed, in the vocabulary of his immediate generation — the appellation 'Aunt' did not necessarily signify a blood relative. It could and did equally well apply to any older woman with whom the family came into close contact.

Not that he was by any means deficient in the genuine article. Wodehouse historian Norman Murphy has traced no less than twenty of them ('As far as the eye could reach, I found myself gazing on a surging sea of aunts. There were tall aunts, short aunts, stout aunts, thin aunts, and an aunt who was carrying on a conversation in a low voice to which nobody seemed to be paying the slightest attention.' (*The Mating Season*). 'Dozens of aunts . . . far-flung aunts scattered all over England, and each the leading blister of her particular county.')

One way or another – whether it was by one or other of the aunts he was to claim he could never remember or by the odd governess or teacher – the Young Wodehouse's early upbringing was very much skewed to the distaff side. And since he was only in his mother's company for some six months between the ages of two and fifteen, all of these 'Aunts' were, for good or ill, mother substitutes. ('Nanny or elder sister . . . you can't ever really lose your awe of someone who used to scrub your face with a soapy flannel.')

Victorian middle-class society being what it was, it was they who would have taken him to church and made him accompany them on formal social visits, thereby giving him early insights into two areas that were to provide him with ample material as a writer in years to come – the upstairs/downstairs world of master and servant and the Great Upstairs as seen from below.

They would also have been likely – almost as a reflex action – to have insisted on strict standards of behaviour. (A Victorian child 'should be seen and not heard'.) Nor would there necessarily have been any great degree of affection involved in the application of the rules. Which is not to suggest that Wodehouse was badly treated by these surrogate mothers – simply that he was denied the maternal love a child needs in its formative years and, as a result, withdrew into a world of his own making, where such things were not allowed to matter. Without embarking on a psychological treatise, it perhaps helps explain his lack of involvement in close personal relationships in later life.

In any case Wodehouse was to have his amiable revenge on the battalions of female authority figures — that 'covey of mildewed females whom he had classified under the general heading of Aunts' ('Goodbye to All Cats' from *Young Men in Spats*).

I suppose the reason why one uses aunts so much as dragons is that one can't very well have an unpleasant mother in a story. I was always very fond of my aunts.

The Wodehouse Aunt *per se* has certain defining characteristics:

. . . A bleak, austere expression. She was looking more like an aunt than anything human. In his boyhood he had observed platoons of aunts with their features frozen in a similar rigidity . . .
(*Barmy in Wonderland*)

*

Aunts as a class are like Napoleon: they expect their orders to be carried out without a hitch and don't listen to excuses.
(*Much Obliged, Jeeves*)

*

Like so many aunts, she was gifted with a sort of second sight.

(*Uncle Fred in the Springtime*)

*

'Barker!' [Freddie's] voice had a ring of pain.
   'Sir?'
   'What's this?'
   'Poached egg, sir.'
   Freddie averted his eyes with a silent shudder.
   'It looks just like an old aunt of mine,' he said.

(*Jill the Reckless*)

*

'Do you know what is the trouble with aunts as a class?'
   'No, sir.'
   'They are not gentlemen.'

(*Aunts Aren't Gentlemen*)

*

When one character casually mentions that he might 'stroll in on' an Aunt, he is firmly dissuaded:

> 'I wouldn't.'
> 'She can't eat me.'
> 'I don't know so much. She's not a veget-
> arian.'
>   (*The Old Reliable*)

By definition, in the Wodehouse canon all young men are doomed to suffer from Aunt-itis but none more so than Bertie Wooster, for whom they assume the proportions of an epidemic:

> In these disturbed days in which we live, it has probably occurred to all thinking men that something drastic ought to be done about aunts. Speaking for myself, I have long felt that stones should be turned and avenues explored with a view to putting a stopper on the relatives in question. If someone were to come to me and say, 'Wooster, would you be interested in joining a society I am starting whose aim will be the suppression of aunts or at least will see to it that they are kept on a short chain and are not permitted to roam hither and thither at will, scattering

desolation on all sides?', I would reply, 'Wilbraham', if his name was Wilbraham, 'I am with you heart and soul. Put me down as a foundation member.'

('Jeeves Makes an Omelette' from *A Few Quick Ones*)

'If I had to start my life again, Jeeves, I would start it as an orphan without any aunts. Don't they put aunts in Turkey in sacks and drop them in the Bosphorus?'

'Odalisques, sir, I understand. Not aunts.'

'Well, why not aunts? Look at the trouble they cause in the world. I tell you, Jeeves . . . behind every poor, innocent, harmless blighter who is going down for the third time in the soup, you will find, if you look carefully enough, the aunt who shoved him into it.'

(*The Code of the Woosters*)

His vision of Aunts *en masse* is of 'Aunt calling to Aunt like mastodons bellowing across primeval swamps' but most of his personal soup is whipped up by two particular Aunts – the Good Witch (Aunt Dahlia) and the Wicked Witch (Aunt Agatha).

'There came from without the hoof-beats of a galloping relative and Aunt Dahlia whizzed in' (*The Code of the Woosters*).

She is described as having a somewhat florid complexion. 'Even at normal times [her] map tended a little towards the crushed strawberry' but now 'she looked like a tomato struggling for self-expression' (*Right Ho, Jeeves*). She 'has a carrying voice . . . If all other sources of income failed, she could make a good living calling the cattle home across the Sands of Dee' (*Very Good, Jeeves*). 'I believe that Aunt Dahlia in her prime could lift fellow members of the Quorn and Pitchley out of their saddles with a single yip, though separated from them by two ploughed fields and a spinney' (*Jeeves in the Offing*). As for her laugh – 'she guffawed more liberally than I had ever heard a woman guffaw. If there had been an aisle, she would have rolled in it . . . She was giving the impression of a hyena which had just heard a good one from another hyena.' (*Much Obliged, Jeeves*).

Bertie was known to cower before her 'like a wet sock' and he was by no means in a minority of one.

'[She] can turn in a flash into a carbon copy of a Duchess of the old school reducing an underling to a spot of grease, and what is so remarkable is that she doesn't have to use a lorgnette, just does it all with the power of the human eye.'

(*Much Obliged, Jeeves*)

And this is his *favourite* aunt!

'The whole trouble is due to your blasted aunt,' said young Bingo.

'Which blasted aunt? Specify, old thing, I have so many.'

'Mrs Travers.'

'Oh, no, dash it, old man,' I protested. 'She's the only decent aunt I've got . . .'

Even more formidable looms her sister, Aunt Agatha ('who eats broken bottles and wears barbed wire next to the skin'):

About the only advantage of having an aunt like [Aunt Agatha] is that it makes one travel, thus broadening the mind and enabling one to see new faces.

(*Joy in the Morning*)

[Aunt Agatha's] demeanour was now rather like that of one who, picking daisies on the railway, has just caught the down express in the small of the back.

('Pearls Mean Tears' from *The Inimitable Jeeves*)

Aunt Agatha is like an elephant – not so much to look at, for in appearance she resembles more a well-bred vulture – but because she never forgets.

(*Joy in the Morning*)

I suddenly observed . . . a striking portrait of Aunt Agatha, from the waist upwards . . . It caught my eye and halted me in my tracks as though I had run into a lamp-post. It was the work of one of those artists who reveal the soul of the sitter, and it had revealed so much of Aunt Agatha's soul that for all practical purposes it might have been that danger to traffic in person. Indeed, I came within an ace of saying 'Oh, hullo!' at the same moment when I could have sworn it said 'Bertie!' in that compelling voice which had so often rung in my ears and caused me to curl up in a ball in the hope that a meek subservience would enable me to get off lightly.

(Joy in the Morning)

Aunt Agatha is one of those strong-minded women. She has an eye like a man-eating fish . . . My experience is that when Aunt Agatha wants you to do a thing you do it, or else you find yourself wondering why those fellows in the olden days made such a fuss when they had trouble with the Spanish inquisition.

When I was a kid at school she was always able to turn me inside out with a single glance . . . There's about five-foot-nine of Aunt Agatha, topped off with a beaky nose, an eagle eye and lots of grey hair, and the general effect is pretty formidable.

('Aunt Agatha Speaks Her Mind' from
The Inimitable Jeeves)

Ironically, although he depicts her as the demonic blister on the Wooster heel, Aunt Agatha merely wants him to toe the line by marrying suitably, working for a living and generally adding up to something. It is Dahlia not Agatha who represents the greater threat to Bertie's well-being by continually dragooning him into stealing cow creamers and committing sundry acts of petty larceny.

It is bad to be trapped in a den of slavering aunts, lashing their tails and glaring at you out of their red eyes.

(*The Mating Season*)

On the whole, in the battle to the death between 'Aunt' and 'Nephew' it is hard not to conclude that Wodehouse had the last word.

* * * *

Uncles, on the other hand, are more sympathetic, mainly because – unlike Aunts – they are gentlemen.

The avuncular ideal is undoubtedly Frederick, Lord Ickenham who 'still retained, together with a juvenile waist-line, the bright enthusiasms and the fresh, unspoiled mental outlook of a slightly inebriated undergraduate' . . . 'Though well stricken in years, the old blister becomes on these occasions as young as he feels, which seems to be about twenty-two.' His face also had 'a lurking gleam such as one might discern in the eye of a small boy who has been left alone in the house and knows where the key of the jam cupboard is . . .' (*Uncle Dynamite*).

The ideal Uncle, in pristine condition, is a close approximation to a perpetual child who happens to have picked up a few interesting habits along the way . . .

My uncle George discovered that alcohol was a food well in advance of modern medical thought.

('The Delayed Exit of Claude and Eustace' from *The Inimitable Jeeves*)

Lord Ickenham . . . folded the girl in a warm embrace. It seemed to Pongo, not for the first time, that this man went out of his way to kiss girls.

(*Uncle Fred in the Springtime*)

. . . rarely, if ever, are they an aesthetic adornment . . .

Uncle Tom always looked a bit like a pterodactyl with a secret sorrow.

(*Right Ho, Jeeves*)

. . . while Uncle Alaric occupied another perch in the same aviary . . .

Few coots could have had less hair . . . and any walrus would have been proud to possess the moustache at which he was puffing.

(*Uncle Fred in the Springtime*)

Of paramount importance to the young man about town – in the world according to Wodehouse – was the ability to turn like a worm and sting like a scorpion when an Uncle had gone too far, if you follow me . . .

'I would just like to say this. You are without exception the worst tick and bounder that ever got fatty degeneration of the heart through half a century of gorging food and swilling wine wrenched from the lips of a starving proletariat. You make me sick. You poison the air. Good-bye, Uncle Alaric,' said Ricky, drawing away rather ostentatiously. 'I think that we had better terminate this interview, or I may become brusque.'

(*Uncle Fred in the Springtime*)

* * * *

Wodehouse was never short of the odd real-life brother or two and relations appear to have been generally cordial – which is perhaps why brothers make relatively few appearances in his work and, when they do, tend to get a good press.

As for sisters . . . since he never had one, he felt free to view them both pro and con . . .

Sisters are a mistake, Clarence. You should have set your face against them at the outset.

(*Pigs Have Wings*)

[*33*]

'I am sorry . . . if my eyes are fishy. The fact has not been called to my attention before.'

'I suppose you never had any sisters,' said Sally. 'They would have told you.'

(*The Adventures of Sally*)

*

A strong-willed sister of twelve can establish over a brother of seven a moral ascendancy which lasts a lifetime.

(*Uncle Dynamite*)

. . . and learn the fundamentals of what it eventually takes to be an Aunt at the same time. Of course, when they get to be older, the whole business can become somewhat more complicated . . .

It is a curious law of Nature that the most undeserving brothers always have the best sisters.

(*Uneasy Money*)

CHAPTER THREE

. . . Downstairs
Butlers, Gentlemen's Gentlemen . . .
and so forth

My mind today is fragrant with memories of kindly
footmen and vivacious parlour maids.

One thing I can remember is how fond I was of the various maids who went through the Prince home. It may have given me my liking for the domestic-servant class.

* * * *

One incidental advantage of staying with so many different 'relations' was the view it gave Wodehouse of the distinctive Upstairs/Downstairs world of Victorian family life. Once the boys had been passed from hand to hand, they would frequently accompany the current 'Aunt' ('many of them vicars' wives') on her social calls 'to the local Great House', usually being consigned to the care of the servants 'below stairs'.

In this subterranean kingdom there was a distinct hierarchy in which the Butler was the unquestioned King. When the Staff duly dined it must have been quite a sight to see the Butler offer his arm to the Housekeeper, before leading in the stately procession in ranking order. All of this the young Wodehouse observed, remembered and eventually resurrected.

If I have a fault as a writer, which is very doubtful, I should say that it was a tendency to devote myself a little too closely to the subject of butlers.

(*Louder and Funnier*)

The fact is, butlers have always fascinated me. As a child, I lived on the fringe of the butler belt. As a young man, I was a prominent pest at houses where butlers were maintained. And later I employed butlers. So it might be said that I have never gone off the butler standard. For fifty years I have omitted no word or act to keep these supermen in the forefront of public thought . . . Time, like an ever-rolling stream, bears all its sons away, and even the Edwardian butler has not been immune. He has joined the Great Auk, Mah-Jong and the snows of yesteryear in limbo . . . The real crusted, vintage butler passed away with Edward the Seventh.

And the vintage Butler could indeed be crusted — not to say crusty:

Suddenly the door opened and there stood an august figure, weighing seventeen stone or so on the hoof, with mauve cheeks, three chins, supercilious lips and bulging gooseberry eyes that raked you with a forbidding stare as if you were something the carrion crow had deposited on the doorstep. 'Not at all what we have been accustomed to,' those eyes seem to say.

I was well over thirty before I could convince myself, when paying a social call, that the reason the butler looked at me in that cold and distant way was that it was his normal expression when on duty, and that he did not do it because he suspected that I was over-drawn at the bank, had pressed my trousers under the mattress, and was trying to make last year's hat do for another season.

('Butlers and the Buttled' from *Louder and Funnier*)

By the laws of their guild butlers of the Edwardian epoch were sometimes permitted a quick, short smile, provided it was sar-donic, but never a guffaw.

Beach, the Butler-in-residence at Blandings Castle, is un-doubtedly *primus inter pares* of the species:

Men of Beach's build do not leap from seats. He did, however, rise slowly like a hippo-potamus emerging from a river bank.

(*A Pelican at Blandings*)

*

Beach . . . was a man who had made two chins grow where only one had been before, and his waistcoat swelled like the sail of a racing yacht.

(*Galahad at Blandings*)

In a Wodehouse Butler, corpulence is definitely *de rigeur:*

Keggs . . . looked almost precisely as he had looked a quarter of a century ago. Then he had resembled a Roman emperor who had been doing himself too well on starchy foods. His aspect now was of a somewhat stouter Roman emperor, one who had given up any attempt to watch his calories and liked his potatoes with lots of butter on them.

(*Something Fishy*)

Taken for all in all, however, 'Keggs was merely a passive evil, like toothache or a rainy day.' ('The Good Angel' from *The Man Upstairs*) . . . while Silversmith (uncle to the inimitable Jeeves) 'looked like one of those steel engravings of nineteenth-century statesmen. He had a large bald head and pale, protruding gooseberry eyes . . .' His customary aspect was that of 'a respectful chunk of dough' (*The Mating Season*).

Gooseberries seemed to be in season in the eye department:

[Blizzard] radiated port and popeyed dignity. He had splay feet and three chins, and when he walked his curving waistcoat preceded him like the advance guard of some royal procession.

('High Stakes' from *The Heart of a Goof*)

*

Oakshott was one of those stout, impressive, ecclesiastical butlers . . . you would have put him down as a Bishop in mufti or, at the least, a plenipotentiary at one of the better courts.

('The Come-Back of Battling Billson' from *Lord Emsworth and Others*)

*

Parker . . . stood in the doorway, trying to look as like a piece of furniture as possible — which is the duty of a good butler.

(*The Pothunters*)

A vintage Wodehouse Butler of a good year needs no bush and is impossible to fake:

Binstead was one of those young, sprightly butlers, encountering whom one feels that in the deepest and holiest sense they are not butlers at all, but merely glorified footmen.

(*Pigs Have Wings*)

But even the impassive vintage Butler has emotions which occasionally show through. Beach, that 'solemn procession of one', has his own distinctive way of registering disapproval – 'ice formed on the butler's upper slopes'. And, when seriously discomfited:

> [He] resembled . . . in his general demeanour one of those unfortunate gentlemen in railway station waiting-rooms who, having injudiciously consented at four-thirty to hold a baby for a strange woman, look at the clock and see that it is now six-fifteen and no relief in sight.
>
> (*Heavy Weather*)

The Butler – in various incarnations – weaves a dignified thread through seventy years of Wodehouse fiction and never ceases to fascinate him as a social phenomenon in real life:

> Any man under thirty years of age who tells you that he is not afraid of an English butler lies.
>
> ('The Good Angel' from *The Man Upstairs*)

> To the dramatist the butler is indispensable. Eliminate him and who is to enter rooms at critical moments when, if another word were spoken, the play would end immediately?

Who is to fill the gaps by coming in with the tea-things, telegrams, the evening paper, and cocktails? Who is to explain the plot of the farce at the rise of the curtain?

('Butlers and the Buttled' from *Louder and Funnier*)

It was only in what my biographers will speak of as my second London period — *circa* 1930 — when I was in the chips and an employer of butlers, that I came to know them well and receive their confidence.

By which time he had made the acquaintance of Jeeves, who was not, strictly speaking, a Butler at all but that infinitely higher being – a valet or gentleman's gentleman – the gentleman-in-question, of course, being Bertram Wooster, Esq.

* * * *

Wodehouse was to be questioned incessantly over the years as to the origins of his two most popular characters – of whom more has been written than of any other characters in popular fiction, with the exception of their alter egos – Holmes and Watson.

'I can't remember how I got the name Wooster', he wrote in 1962 to a correspondent of the same name, 'I think it may have been from a serial in the old *Captain*, where one of the characters was called Worcester. The odd thing is that the Bertie Wooster character started out as Reggie Pepper, and I don't know why I changed the name.'

The odd thing is that you haven't a criminal face. It's a silly fatuous face . . . you remind me of one of those fellows who do dances with the soubrette in musical comedy.
(*Much Obliged, Jeeves*)

In 'Comrade Bingo' Bertie is described as 'the tall one with the face like a motor mascot'.

By the time I had written two or three books his character was all clear before me. He's very vivid to me now. Of course, he's altered tremendously. When he first began he was very much the sort of stage dude, he gradually became more and more individual . . . He's picked up a lot of things from Jeeves.

(*Radio Broadcast*)

Not least a smattering of ill-digested erudition:
('True, in the course of years I have picked up a vocabulary of sorts from Jeeves.' Bertie admits.)

It is pretty generally recognised in the circles in which he moves that Bertram Wooster is not a man who lightly throws in the towel and admits defeat. Beneath the thingummies of what d'you call it, his head, wind and weather permitting, is as a rule bloody but unbowed, and if the slings and arrows of outrageous fortune want to crush his proud spirit, they have to pull their socks up and make a special effort.

Bertie Wooster is a fellow whom it is dashed difficult to deceive. Old Lynx-Eye is about what it amounts to. I observe and deduce. I

weigh the evidence and draw my con-
clusions.

It's not all jam writing a story in the first
person. The reader can know nothing except
what Bertie tells him, and Bertie can know
only a limited amount himself.

(Letter to William Townend, 6 March 1932)

He was a little clearer about Jeeves. Having read the American
writer Harry Leon Wilson's novel, *Ruggles of Red Gap*, 'I
remember feeling that he had got the English valet all wrong
. . . I thought he had missed the chap's dignity. I think it was
then that the idea of Jeeves came into my mind.' On the choice
of name he was quite clear. He wrote in a letter to lifelong fan,
Walter Simmons – 'I was watching a county match on the
Cheltenham ground before the first war and one of the
Gloucestershire bowlers was called Jeeves. I suppose the name
stuck in my mind, and I named Jeeves after him.'

The fast bowler was one Percy Jeeves and he was thought to
have England potential. Unfortunately, he was to die at Flanders
in 1916. Wodehouse took only his surname, giving Jeeves (as
late as 1971 the rarely used Christian name of 'Reginald'. (On
a point of detail, he also misremembered his county affiliation.
Jeeves actually played for Warwickshire *against* Gloucestershire.)

As for a real-life role model, Wodehouse was to admit in a
late letter to Guy Bolton that he had misled his friend on the
matter: 'When we did *Bring on the Girls,* if you remember, I said
that I drew Jeeves from a butler I had called Robinson. Untrue,

of course. At the start I had no model for him except the conventional stage butler.' (Another Wodehouse contradiction here, for at a 1920s London dinner party – 'buttled' by the aforesaid Robinson – he was heard to tell Bolton that the man was an author's model and 'a walking *Encyclopaedia Britannica*'. Incidentally, it is interesting to note that the Jeeves of the novels from 1934 onwards was more demonstrably knowledgeable even than the Jeeves of the earlier short stories.)

Little is recorded of Jeeves's early history, though it seems likely that he, too, saw action. When asked by Lord Rowcester: 'Were you in the First World War, Jeeves?' Jeeves replies, 'I dabbled in it to a certain extent, m'lord.' From his first job – as pageboy at a girls' school – he was at various times in service with Lord Worplesdon, Mr Digby Thistleton (later Lord Bridgnorth), Montague Todd, Lord Brancaster, Lord Frederick Ranelagh (with Lord Rowcester and Lord Chufnell among later temporary postings) – before Fate brought him into the life of the Young Master:

I started writing in 1902 and every day I said to myself, 'I must get a character for a series.' In 1916 I wrote the first Jeeves story. About a year later I wrote another. But it wasn't until I had done about six at long intervals that I realised I had got a series-character.

I find it curious, now that I have written so much about him, to recall how softly and undramatically Jeeves first entered my little world. On that occasion he spoke just two lines. The first was: 'Mrs Gregson to see you, sir.' The second, 'Very good, sir. Which suit will you wear?' . . . It was only some time later . . . that the man's qualities dawned upon me. I still blush to think of the off-hand way I treated him at our first encounter.

(Introduction to *The Jeeves Omnibus*)

At their first meeting a hungover Bertie opens the door of his flat
. . . 'A kind of darkish sort of respectful Johnnie stood
without.' Bertie tells him to 'stagger in, and he floated
noiselessly through the doorway like a healing zephyr . . . This
fellow didn't seem to have any feet at all. He just streamed in.
He had a grave, sympathetic face . . .' ('Jeeves Takes Charge'
from *Carry On, Jeeves*).

As the character of Jeeves evolved, he steadily acquired the
characteristics by which we now know him.

> 'Jeeves is a wonder.'
> 'A marvel.'
> 'What a brain.'
> 'Size nine-and-a-quarter, I should say.'
> 'He eats a lot of fish.''
>   (*Thank You, Jeeves*)

There was his marked discretion . . .

> It was the soft cough of Jeeves's which always
> reminds me of the very old sheep clearing its
> throat on a distant mountain top.'
>   (*Stiff Upper Lip, Jeeves*)

> . . . a low, gentle cough like a sheep with a
> blade of grass in its throat.
>   ('The Great Sermon Handicap' from *The Inimitable Jeeves*)

. . . his virtual invisibility . . .

Jeeves entered – or perhaps one should say shimmered into the room . . . tall and dark and impressive . . .

(*Ring for Jeeves*)

[He resembled] the High Priest of some refined and dignified religion . . .

One of the rummy things about Jeeves is that, unless you watch like a hawk, you very seldom see him come into a room. He's like one of those weird birds in India who dissolve themselves into thin air and nip through space in a sort of disembodied way and assemble the parts again just where they want them.

('The Artistic Career of Corky' from *Carry On, Jeeves*)

. . . the imperturbability . . .

Jeeves doesn't exactly smile on these occasions, because he never does, but the lips twitch slightly at the corners and the eye is benevolent.

(*Joy in the Morning*)

[He] smiled paternally. Or, rather, he had a kind of paternal muscular spasm about the mouth, which is the nearest he ever gets to smiling.

('The Artistic Career of Corky' from *Carry On, Jeeves*)

The corner of his mouth curved quite a quarter of an inch, and for a moment his eye ceased to look like a meditative fish's

('The Aunt and the Sluggard')

. . . and, of course, eating all that fish explains the excess of grey matter – not to mention the way his head sticks out at the back. ('Jeeves let his brain out another notch' – *The Mating Season*).

'Tell me, were you always like this or did it come on suddenly?'

'Sir?'

'The brain. The grey matter. Were you an outstandingly brilliant boy?'

'My mother thought me intelligent, sir.'

'You can't go by that. My mother thought *me* intelligent.'

('Episode of the Dog McIntosh' from *Very Good, Jeeves*)

Which raises the question of Jeeves's age and physical appearance. In the late 1960s Wodehouse and his longtime collaborator, Guy Bolton, were contemplating a Bertie–Jeeves musical. Wodehouse was doubtful about a 'Singing Jeeves', although perhaps 'it would be all right with Stanley Holloway as Jeeves'. The problem, as he saw it, was that 'people have got such a fixed idea of Jeeves as an elderly, grave, rotund character'. Yet, if that were so – and since neither Jeeves nor Bertie age a smidgen from the beginning of the saga to the end – it is most unlikely that Jeeves could have established 'understandings' with 'young persons' from other establishments, when a Wooster gaffe required covert action on his part. A permanent and virile middle age would seem to be indicated.

The musical – had it ever been staged – would have sidestepped the one limitation of the 'subjective camera' technique Wodehouse employs in exploring the World According to Wooster. We can only see what Bertie sees. At what it *means* we must guess. On stage and through song Jeeves can and must express himself to us directly.

In a song called 'Lament of a Gentleman's Gentleman' he worries about where the Young Master's ineptitude will lead them both.

> *It's hard on a gentleman's gentleman*
> *Whose employer from dignity slips,*
> *And day after day*
> *Behaves in a way*
> *That makes his best friends purse their lips.*
> *He feels like a loving parental man*
> *With a son whom he can't but deplore;*
> *For it's woe for a gentleman's gentleman,*
> *It's a blow for a gentleman's gentleman*

When a gentleman's gentleman's gentleman
Is not a gentleman any more!

He himself is often tempted to return to his ancestral roots in Brixton but — *noblesse oblige*:

The voice of duty calls on me to stay:
As Mr Wooster says, I'm bound
To stick it out and rally round
When he's so deeply in the consommé.
If I were to desert my post
Precisely when he needs me most,
A breach of feudal spirit it would seem,
So on the whole I think it best
To say once more 'J'y suis, J'y reste'
And Brixton must remain a golden dream.

Even though Jeeves bails Bertie out of more *bouillon* than master chef Anatole could shake a ladle at, the Young Master's gratitude is often at a premium.

There are aspects of Jeeves's character which have frequently caused coldness to arise between us. He is one of those fellows who, if you give them a thingummy, take a what-d'you-call-it. His work is often raw, and he has been known to allude to me as 'mentally negligible'. More than once it has been my painful task to squelch in him a tendency to get uppish and treat the young master as a serf or peon. These are grave defects.

(*Right Ho, Jeeves*)

I was dashed if I was going to let Jeeves treat me like a bally one man chain-gang.

('Jeeves and the Unbidden Guest' from *Carry On, Jeeves*)

To which Jeeves – who had always softened 'mentally somewhat negligible' with 'but he has a heart of gold' – predictably responds:

'Yes, sir,' said Jeeves in a low, cold voice, as if he had been bitten in the leg by a personal friend.

('Clustering Round Young Bingo' from *Carry On, Jeeves*)

These are mere straws, Jeeves. Do not let us chop them.

(*Right Ho, Jeeves*)

After such a rift in the lute, Jeeves invariably manages to delete some offending item of attire from Bertie's wardrobe:

Jeeves lugged my purple socks out of the
drawer as if he were a vegetarian fishing a
caterpillar out of his salad.

('Jeeves and the Chump Cyril' from *My Man Jeeves*)

. . . or manoeuvre to remove an offending temporary growth of
facial hair. He describes one of Bertie's two recorded
moustaches as looking like 'a stain of mulligatawny soup on the
upper lip'.

'Very good,' I said coldly. 'In that case,
tinkerty-tonk.' And I meant it to sting.

(*Right Ho, Jeeves*)

When two men of iron will live in close
association with one another, there are
bound to be occasional clashes.

(*The Code of the Woosters*)

Fortunately, it won't be long before Jeeves is once again making the world safe for the Young Master to inhabit:

'And thus the native hue of resolution is sicklied o'er in the pale cast of thought, and enterprises of great pith and moment with this regard their currents turn awry and lose the name of action.'

'Exactly, you took the words right out of my mouth.'

(*The Code of the Woosters*)

'Do you know, Jeeves, you're – well, you absolutely stand alone!'

'I endeavour to give satisfaction, sir,' said Jeeves.

If there is a chance that suavity will ease a situation, the Woosters always give it a buzz.

(*Joy in the Morning*)

* * * *

Jeeves knows his place and it is between the covers of a book.

(Introduction to *The Jeeves Omnibus*)

CHAPTER FOUR

Dulwich

The fashionable thing is to look back and hate your
school, but I loved Dulwich . . . I always had a
good time there.

The most deadly error mortal man can make, with
the exception of calling a school a college, is to
call a college a school.

(The Pothunters)

'You don't know anything about anything,' Mr
Pynsent pointed out gently. 'It's the effect of your
English public school education.'

(Sam the Sudden)

To me the years between 1896 and 1900
seem like Heaven. Was the average man
really unhappy at school? Or was Dulwich in
our time an exceptionally good school?

(Letter to William Townend, 7 March 1946)

* * * *

From 2 May 1894, when he first passed through the gates of
Dulwich College as a pupil, until he left six years later,
Wodehouse felt at home for the first time in his life.

Founded in 1619 by the celebrated Elizabethan actor Edward
Alleyn – a contemporary of Shakespeare – it was originally
known as Alleyn's College of God's Gift. By Wodehouse's time
the Upper School was known as Dulwich College and the
Lower School as Alleyn's School.

It was what you would call a middle-class
school. We were all the sons of reasonably
solvent but certainly not wealthy parents,
and we all had to earn our living later on.
Compared with Eton, Dulwich would be
something like an American State University
compared with Harvard or Princeton. Bertie
Wooster's parents would never have sent
him to Dulwich, but Ukridge could very well
have been there.

Later he would have his own fun with some of the alternative establishments:

> Mr Bodkin, miss, so I understand from the ties in his drawer, was educated at Eton. That's where he's handicapped in these matters.
>
> *(The Luck of the Bodkins)*

> 'Didn't Frankenstein get married?'
>
> 'Did he?' said Eggy. 'I don't know. I never met him. Harrow man, I expect.'
>
> *(Laughing Gas)*

> The average parent chose the Classical 'side', where [their sons] learned Latin and Greek, presumably with a vague idea that if all went well they would go to Oxford or Cambridge. In my day, to the ordinary parent, education meant Classics. I went automatically to the Classical side and, as it turned out, it was the best form of education I could have had as a writer.

The fact that older brother Armine was already firmly ensconced and making a name for himself was something of a mixed blessing but it made little difference in the long run. ('Armine and I were always good friends . . . there was never any feeling of rivalry between us.') Armine was the more academic and Wodehouse the more athletic. He was in the school cricket team for two years, the football team for one and was considered a fair boxer until that iffy eyesight once more made its presence felt.

* * * *

Cricket became a source of recurrent imagery in his fiction for the rest of his life:

There would have been serious trouble between David and Jonathan if either had persisted in dropping catches off the other's bowling.

(*Jackson Junior* or *Mike at Wrykyn* — the first half of *Mike*)

There was the umpire with his hands raised, as if he were the Pope bestowing a blessing.

('Tom, Dick and Harry' in *Grand Magazine*)

He gave me the sort of look a batsman gives an umpire when he gives him out leg-before-wicket.

('Concealed Art' in *Strand Magazine*)

To American readers cricket is, of course, a sealed book. What puzzles them is how a game can go on for five days . . . Would not the two teams, they ask, have been better occupied staying at home with a good book? Why, in the time it takes to get through the normal England v. Australia game you could read the whole of Shakespeare's output and quite a good deal of Erle Stanley Gardner's.

(Introduction to US edition of *Mike at Wrykyn*)

* * * *

In later life golf became Wodehouse's game of choice – a game he pursued with rather more enthusiasm than skill, as he was the first to admit:

For an untouchable like myself two perfect drives in a round would wipe out all memory of sliced approach shots and foozled putts, whereas if Jack Nicklaus does a sixty-four he goes home and thinks morosely that if he had not just missed that eagle on the seventh, he would have had a sixty-three.

(Introduction to *The Golf Omnibus*)

He had, it appeared, only one *caveat in re* the noble game – the Saturday foursome!

I am not an arrogant man. I am not one of those golfers who despise all humanity whose handicap is in double figures. If I ever find a worse player than myself – I have not done so yet – I shall pity him, not despise him. But, whatever you may say against my style of play, however much you may animadvert against my stance, my grip, and the buoyant manner in which I toss my head in the air – like a lion of the desert scenting his prey – just before my club descends on the ball, at least you must admit this in my favour, that there are not four of me.

I may be a rotten exponent of the Royal and Ancient: I will even concede a point by admitting that I am a bally rotten exponent: but at any rate I play alone as a rule, and, playing alone, have no standing. If I overtake people, I wait; if they overtake me, I withdraw into the undergrowth until they have whizzed by. In other words, my bad play is my own affair and does nobody any harm.

In the 1930s he played quite often with his friend, the thriller writer E. Phillips Oppenheim, who remembered that 'Plum Wodehouse's golf . . . was of a curious fashion. He had only one idea in his mind when he took up his stance on the tee, and that idea was length . . . he went for the ball with one of the most comprehensive and vigorous swings I have ever seen. I am certain that I saw him hit a ball once which was the longest shot I have ever seen in my life without any trace of following wind.

'You will never see that again!' I remarked, after my first gasp of astonishment, mingled, I am afraid I must confess, with a certain amount of malevolent pleasure as the ball disappeared in the bosom of a huge clump of gorse.

'I wonder how far it was,' was the wistful reply.

Later that evening Wodehouse's caddie arrived with the missing ball. 'Got the distance?' Wodehouse asked eagerly. 'Three hundred and forty-three yards, sir,' the caddie replied promptly.

There was a glow of happiness in P.G.'s expression.

'Beaten my own record by five yards,' he confided with a grin.

'But listen,' I pointed out, 'how many matches do you win?'

'I never win a match,' was the prompt reply. 'I spend my golfing life out of bounds. I never even count my strokes . . . All the same I get more fun out of my golf than any other man I know when I am hitting my drives.'

And he certainly *gave* more fun to any golfer capable of seeing the funny side of their particular religion:

It was a morning when all nature shouted 'Fore!' The breeze, as it blew gently up from the valley, seemed to bring a message of hope and cheer, whispering of chip-shots holed and brassies landing squarely on the meat.

('The Heart of a Goof' from *The Heart of a Goof*)

* * * *

Reggie's was a troubled spirit these days. He was in love, and he had developed a bad slice with his mid-iron. He was practically a soul in torment.

(*A Damsel in Distress*)

* * * *

'After all, golf is only a game,' said Millicent. Women say these things without thinking. It does not mean that there is any kink in their character. They simply don't realise what they are saying.

('Ordeal By Golf' from *The Clicking of Cuthbert*)

* * * *

It is an excellent thing that women should be encouraged to take up golf . . . Golf humanises women, humbling their haughty natures, tends, in short, to knock out of their systems a certain modicum of that super-ciliousness, that swank, which makes wooing such a tough proposition for the diffident male.

('The Rough Stuff' from *The Clicking of Cuthbert*)

* * * *

Most divorces spring from the fact that the husband is too markedly superior to his wife at golf; this leading him, when she starts criticising his relations, to say bitter and unforgivable things about her mashie-shots.

('Rodney Fails to Qualify' from *The Heart of a Goof*)

* * * *

The least thing upsets him on the links. He missed short putts because of the uproar of the butterflies in the adjoining meadows.

('Ordeal by Golf' from *The Clicking of Cuthbert*)

* * * *

The fourth hole found him four down, and one had the feeling that he was lucky not to be five.

('Excelsior!' from *Nothing Serious*)

* * * *

There are few better things in life than a public school summer term . . . The freedom of it after . . . even the most easy-going private school, is intoxicating.

(*Jackson Junior* or *Mike at Wrykyn*)

Being a solidly-built young man, he may well have avoided some of the ragging that new boys at a public school invariably face.

In *Mike*, one of his later school stories, though, he can summon up some of the *angst* involved, as well as parody the form:

> In stories of the 'Not Really a Duffer' type, where the nervous new boy, who has been found crying in the boot-room over the photograph of his sister, contrives to get an innings in the game, nobody suspects that he is really a prodigy till he hits the Bully's first ball out of the ground for six.
> (Chapter 40)

> Are you the Bully, the Pride of the School, or the Boy who is Led Astray and Takes to Drink in Chapter Sixteen?'
> (Chapter 32)

. . . to which Mike Jackson replies –

> 'The last, for choice, but I've only just arrived, so I don't know.'
> (*The Lost Lambs* or *Mike and Psmith* from *Mike*)

Because of his parents' peripatetic lifestyle, Wodehouse was by turns boarder and day boy but he infinitely preferred being a boarder, because 'it offered much more opportunity for making friendships and generally feeling that one was part of the life of the school . . .' Although, as he later recalled, 'I was pretty friendly with everybody but I had no intimate friends.' (The exception he overlooked was William 'Bill' Townend with whom he shared a room for just over a year and with whom he corresponded for the next fifty. Their letters were to form the basis for *Performing Flea*).

> We were a great all-round school in those days . . . The brainless athlete was quite a rarity. We might commit mayhem on the football field, but after the game was over we trotted off to our houses and wrote Latin verse.

For the first few years he applied himself to his books and there is no doubt that his grasp of languages acquired in these years taught him a great deal about the origins and construction of the English language. In his fiction he prefers to play with his erudition but before you can play, you have to know what you are playing with. The classical education is there for all to see but made palatable by the hoops Wodehouse sends it jumping through.

Though Latin and Greek were his main subjects, there was also French . . .

> Into the face of the young man who sat on the terrace of the Hotel Magnifique at Cannes there had crept a look of furtive shame, the shifty, hangdog look that announces that an Englishman is about to talk French.
>
> (*The Luck of the Bodkins*)

'Do you speak French fluently?'

'Very, what I know of it. Which is just that word, *l'addition* and, of course, *Oo, là, là!*'

(*Something Fishy*)

I never succeeded in speaking French but I learned to read it all right . . . I stuck to the normal grunts and gurgles of the foreigner who finds himself cornered by anything Gallic.

(Introduction to *French Leave*)

He also found the currency a little confusing . . .

I went down to the town [Le Touquet] to buy some stamps yesterday and tried to pay the woman at the shop with a piece of toilet paper, which I thought was a fifty franc bill. She laughed heartily . . .

(Letter to Leonora Wodehouse, 19 December 1934)

It is what the French would call an *impasse*. In fact, it is what the French *do* call an *impasse*. Only they say *ahm-parrse*. Silly, of course, but you know what Frenchmen are.

'What asses these Frenchmen are! Why can't
they talk English?'

'They are possibly more to be pitied than
censured, m'lord. Early upbringing no doubt
has a lot to do with it.'

(*Ring For Jeeves*)

* * * *

The Headmaster during Wodehouse's time was A. H. Gilkes,
one of the legendary Victorian headmasters, comparable, say,
with Rugby's Dr Arnold. 'He was a man with a long white beard
who stood six-foot-six in his socks and he had one of those deep
musical voices . . . he also always scared the pants off me.'

Which perhaps goes some way to explain his cathartic
treatment of his fictional headmasters:

The Rev. Aubrey was taking the senior class
in Bible history, and when a headmaster has
got his teeth into a senior class, he does not
readily sheathe the sword.

('Bramley is So Bracing' from *Nothing Serious*)

From the fact that he spoke as if he had a hot
potato in his mouth without getting the
raspberry from the lads in the ringside seats,
I deduced that he must be the headmaster.

(*Right Ho, Jeeves*)

He was later to parody Gilkes — a man not over-given to encouraging his pupils:

So you made a century against Tonbridge, did you, my boy? Well, always remember that you will soon be dead, and in any case, the bowling was probably rotten.

In retrospect his view of Gilkes became ambivalent and he concluded that perhaps, after all, the man had not been consistently stern *enough*:

Boys respect strength, nothing but strength. They may dislike it, but they respect it. A school is like a child. The mother who alternately spoils and storms at a child makes it unmanageable. Same with headmaster and school.

Armine won a scholarship to Oxford and once again it looked as though Wodehouse was about to tread in his brother's steps. At which point reality bit.

The ever-temperamental rupee took a nosedive, causing Wodehouse Senior to conclude that 'two sons at the university would be a son more than the privy purse could handle. So Learning drew the loser's end, and Commerce got me.'

He writes to his friend, Eric George – 'Friend of me boyhood, here is some dread news for you. My people have not got enough of what are vulgarly but forcibly called "stamps" to send me to Varsity . . . Oh! Money, money, thy name is money! (a most lucid remark).'

Not surprisingly, the disappointment caused him to take his foot off the academic pedal. In the summer term of 1899 he came twenty-fourth in his Classics class – which might not have been so bad, had there been more than twenty-five in the class . . . Instead, he concentrated on his other interests, becoming one of the five editors of the school magazine, *The Alleynian*, to which he continued to contribute for the rest of his life.

The legacy of Dulwich is impossible to pin down in concrete terms but it would be fair to see the basic public-school values of fair play, loyalty and honesty reflected in the writings of the next seventy years – the Code of the Wodehouses. That and the conviction that, as long as one abided by the rules of the game, a chap should be left to do whatever he wanted to do – in his case, write.

Dulwich provided the first stable society Wodehouse had ever known. In a sense he never left it . . .

* * * *

'Travel is highly educational, sir.'
'I can't do with any more education. I was full up years ago.'
(*The Code of the Woosters*)

Even so, there was to be one glorious moment in the academic sun, when in 1939 Oxford University gave him the acclaim that Dulwich had withheld in the form of an honorary degree . . .

I had a great time at Oxford. I stayed with the Vice-Chancellor, who is a splendid chap, and enjoyed every minute of it. Did Victor tell you that I rolled up to the Christ Church dinner in a black tie, to find four hundred gorgeous beings in white tie and decorations? It never occurred to me that an all-men dinner would be white tie. However, the robes hid my shame quite a bit. They were dove-grey and scarlet – very dressy. I had to wear them all day, and was sorry I couldn't go round in them in private life. They certainly do give one an air.

(Letter to Molly Cazalet, 10 July 1939)

CHAPTER FIVE

Uneasy Money

The Autumn of 1900, when, a comely youth of some eighteen summers, I accepted employment in the Lombard Street office of the Hong Kong and Shanghai Bank. Reluctantly, I may mention. As the song says – 'I didn't want to do it, I didn't want to do it', but my hand was forced.

I must ask you in future to try and synchronise your arrival at the office with that of the rest of the staff. We aim as far as possible at the communal dead heat.

(*Ice in the Bedroom*)

* * * *

After Dulwich Wodehouse's idea of a good time would have been to linger in the parental Shropshire nest and write – something he was now beginning to do in earnest, though without marked commercial success. Wodehouse Senior, however, was a firm believer in the work ethic – even though he was no longer driven by it himself. He used his Asian contacts to secure a position at the bank . . .

I do not blame [my parents] for feeling that a son in a bank making his £80 a year, just like finding it in the street, was a sounder commercial proposition than one living at home and spending a fortune on stamps [to publishers].

I have always thought it illustrative of the haphazard methods of education in the nineties . . . that I should have been put on the Classical side at Dulwich and taught to write Greek and Latin verse and so on when

I was going to wind up in a bank. I had had absolutely no training for commerce, and right through my two years at the bank I never had the slightest inkling of what banking was. I simply could not understand what was going on.

There were only two things connected with Higher Finance that I really understood. One was that from now on all that I would be able to afford in the way of lunch would be a roll and butter and a cup of coffee, a discovery which, after the lavish midday meals of school, shook me to my foundations. The other was that if I got to the office late three mornings in a month, I would lose my Christmas bonus. One of the great sights of the City in the years 1901–02 was me rounding into the straight with my coat-tails flying and just about making it across the threshold while thousands cheered. It kept me in superb condition, and gave me a rare appetite for the daily roll and butter.

In one of his first novels, *Psmith in the City* (1910), he has his archetypal schoolboy hero, Mike Jackson — a loosely

autobiographical character from earlier school stories – tread
the same precarious path:

> Inside, the bank seemed to be in a state of
> some confusion. Men were moving about in
> an apparently irresolute manner. Nobody
> seemed actually to be working . . . As he
> stood near the doorway, one or two panting
> figures rushed up the steps, and flung
> themselves at a large book which stood on the
> counter near the door. Mike was to come to
> know this book well. In it, if you were an
> employee of the New Asiatic Bank, you had
> to inscribe your name every morning. It was
> removed at ten sharp to the accountant's
> room . . .

There were, admittedly, compensations in the cameraderie of
people working together for a common purpose, 'something
akin to, though a thousand times weaker than, the public school
spirit. Such a community lacks the main motive of the public
school spirit, which is pride in the school and its achievements.
Nobody can be proud of the achievements of a bank.'

However, Wodehouse was to make a name for himself in
banking circles – of sorts . . .

> Possibly because I was a dedicated literary
> artist with a soul above huckstering or

possibly – and this was the view more widely held in the office – because I was just a plain dumb brick, I proved to be the most inefficient clerk whose trouser seat ever polished the surface of a high stool.

He was shunted from the Postal Department – where he found sticking stamps onto letters reasonably congenial, if not mentally taxing, work – to Inward Bills to Outward Bills to Cash . . . 'always with a weak, apologetic smile on my face and hoping that suavity of manner would see me through . . . my total inability to grasp what was going on made me something of a legend in the place'. He imagined the legacy and reputation that would follow him down the corridor of the years . . . 'You should have seen P.G. Wodehouse. Ah, they don't make them like that nowadays. They've lost the pattern.'

*

They train bank clerks to stifle emotion, so that they will be able to refuse overdrafts when they become managers.

('Ukridge's Accident Syndicate' from *Ukridge*)

*

The whole secret of success, if you were running a business and had Monty Bodkin working for you, was to get rid of him at the earliest possible moment.

(*Heavy Weather*)

*

'If you were not handicapped by a public school . . . education,' he said, 'I could suggest many professions. But I fear that your upbringing has hardly fitted you for them. There is the Church, of course.'

('The Pro' from *Pearsons Magazine,* August 1906)

* * * *

Essentially, Lombard Street was a branch office which trained promising young men for a couple of years before sending them off to the Far East to manage one of the bank's subsidiaries. ('They are put to work when young, and they stay put. They are mussels. Each has his special place on the rock, and remains glued to it all his life' – *The Girl on the Boat*.)

The prospect of being transported East of Suez appalled Wodehouse: 'The picture of myself managing a branch was one I preferred not to examine too closely. I couldn't have managed a whelk-stall.'

He was saved by what psychiatrists would undoubtedly see as an act of self-immolation. One day, on being given a pristine new ledger, this man who could not stop writing found himself using that first blank page to write a fantasy about the opening of a new ledger. He was well into it before he realised the heinous nature of his crime – he had Defaced A Ledger. It was the work of a moment to neatly remove the offending page but a *dénouement* was at hand.

A minor war ensued between the Head Cashier and the printer who had provided the ledger. The list of suspects was short to the point of containing only one name. It was the most dramatic thing that happened to him in the world of finance . . . ('It was immediately after this that I found myself at liberty to embark on the life literary.')

* * * *

Fortunately, his real interests now showed signs of being profitable in their own way. All through his two years in the bank, Wodehouse had been writing non-stop. Sometimes on the bank's time and always on his own in his 'horrible lodgings . . . off the King's Road'.

'I wrote everything in those days . . . verses, short stories, articles for the lowest type of weekly paper – only a small proportion of them ever reaching print.' Nonetheless, he managed to place some eighty pieces. The prospect of the waiting whelk-stall was only one reason he was not looking forward to being sent to the East . . . 'The other, of course, was that I wanted to abandon commerce and earn my living as a writer, and I felt that this could be done only by remaining in London. The cross all young writers have to bear is that, while they know that they are going to be spectacularly successful some day, they find it impossible to convince their nearest and dearest that they will ever amount to a row of beans.' He felt from the moment he joined the bank that he had two years 'to establish myself on a pinnacle of fame as a writer'.

Midway through his brief tenure at the bank Wodehouse contracted mumps and retired to utilise the recuperation at his parents' Shropshire home. 'I went back to my people to have them there. I wrote nineteen short stories in three weeks, I just sent the stories out . . . (all of which, I regret to say, editors were compelled to decline owing to lack of space. The editors regretted it, too. They said so.)'

'They were awful. And to make matters worse, they were all written in longhand. My trouble, as with all beginning authors, was that I did not know how to write.' He collected rejection slips and 'some of them were rather pretty' . . . 'I could have papered the walls of a good-sized banqueting hall' . . . 'But what I always feel about rejection slips is that their glamour soon wears off. When you've seen one, I often say, you've seen them all.' . . . 'Worse bilge than mine may have been submitted to the editors of London in 1901 and 1902, but I should think it very unlikely.'

Three weeks' intensive practice may or may not have helped his style but it may well have affected his future content. Mumps is one of the most undermining illnesses that can plague an adult male and it almost certainly left Wodehouse sterile and possibly impotent. Several of his biographers have speculated that this fact alone may account for the asexuality of his subsequent characters and storylines.

* * * *

Although he did not know it at the time, his eventual salvation was at hand.

The Globe was an evening paper with a hundred-year history. Its popular 'By the Way' column was currently being run by one Harold Begbie, assisted by William Beach-Thomas, whom Wodehouse had known as a master at Dulwich. The connection was enough to cause Wodehouse to pay him a visit . . .

I went to see Beach-Thomas to ask if he could get me any work, and he said that he and Begbie often wanted to take a day off and would be glad of somebody who would fill in for them. The payment was ten shillings and sixpence per day.

He would earn his money. Writing the 'By the Way' column involved continuous topicality. 'You would quote something from the morning paper and then you'd make some comment on it. You learnt to skim the news and see things, well, wrong way up, perhaps, for jokes . . . It was always the same type of joke. Nobody had altered that formula in all the fifty years of [the column's] existence. And that was only the start.' Over the on-and-off seven years he was associated with the column, 'I used to have to write a set of verses every morning between ten-thirty and twelve . . . six days a week. It was a discipline, you had to get it done.'

During his time at the bank, when the call came from Beach-Thomas, Wodehouse would find himself suffering from 'non-existent attacks of neuralgia' – but somehow he managed the balancing act and gained valuable professional experience in writing to a deadline.

Then – in September 1902 – Beach-Thomas told him that he needed someone to hold the fort for him while he took a five-week vacation. Was Wodehouse interested? 'On September 9th,' he confided to his diary, 'having to choose between *The Globe* and the bank, I chucked the latter and started out on my wild lone as a freelance. This month starts my journalistic career.' By the end of the year he had earned £65. 6s. 7d.

In August 1903 he was offered and accepted a more permanent job by taking over the column and of that period he would write:

In my early twenties it would not be too much to say that I was the talk of London. If you had not seen me riding my bicycle down The Strand to the offices of *The Globe* . . . frequently using no hands and sometimes bending over to pick up a handkerchief with my teeth, it was pretty generally agreed that you had not seen anything. And the public's memory must be very short if the 22 not out I made for the printers of *The Globe* against the printers of the *Evening News* one Sunday in

1904 has been forgotten . . . I was leaving footprints on the sands of time, and good large footprints at that.

If he ever had any second thoughts, they were humorous ones . . .

I do sometimes find myself wondering if I might not have done better on leaving the Hong Kong and Shanghai Bank to have bought a black mask and an ounce or two of trinitrotoluol and chanced my arm as a member of the underworld. When I see how well some of these underworld chaps are doing . . . it is hard not to feel that they are on the right lines.

Despite the number of times he issued a *caveat* or entered a *nolle prosequi*, he would insist in later life – 'I enjoyed my two years at the bank enormously.'

* * * *

Perhaps one should put it down to the 'cock-eyed' comic vision of his that turned everything around until its funny side was showing, but Wodehouse in print had very little time for other professions than the one that had sought him out.

The legal profession was invariably shifty . . .

He came in now in that wary manner peculiar to lawyers, looking from side to side as if expecting to see torts and malfeasances hiding behind the curtains and misdemeanours under the piano.

(*If I Were You*)

*

The two lawyers then left, chatting amiably about double burgage, heirs taken in socage, and the other subjects which always crop up when lawyers get together.

(*Big Money*)

*

That's what comes of being a solicitor, it saps the vital juices. [He] doesn't even embezzle his clients' money, which I should have thought was about the only fun a solicitor can get out of life.

(*Ice in the Bedroom*)

. . . and as for the police — well, what could you expect of people who couldn't take a joke when a chap knocked their helmet off on Boat Race Night . . . ?

The Sergeant of Police . . . was calm, stolid and ponderous, giving the impression of being constructed of some form of suet.

(*Frozen Assets*)

*

Some policemen are born grafters, some achieve graft and some have graft thrust upon them.

(*Aunts Aren't Gentlemen*)

Then there was the Stock Exchange . . .

A youth and middle age spent on the London Stock Exchange had left Lester Carmody singularly broad-minded. He had to a remarkable degree that precious charity which allows a man to look indulgently on any financial project, however fishy, provided he can see a bit in it for himself.

(*Money for Nothing*)

. . . Accountants . . .

All chartered accountants have hearts as big as hotels. You think they're engrossed in auditing the half-yearly balance sheet of

Miggs, Montagu and Murgatroyd, general importers, and all the time they're writing notes to blondes saying 'Tomorrow, one-thirty, same place.'

(*Ice in the Bedroom*)

. . . and the Civil Service . . .

'He'll probably be an ambassador some day.'
  'Thus making a third world war inevitable.'

(*Frozen Assets*)

. . . and Politics . . .

He's got about as much intelligence as a
Cabinet minister.

(*Much Obliged, Jeeves*)

Practically all Governments ought to be in
Colney Hatch [mental hospital].

(Letter to William Townend, 15 January 1949)

. . . not to mention those new-fangled Psychiatrist fellows . . .

'. . . a psychiatrist.'

'A what?'

'One of those fellows who ask you
questions about your childhood and gradually
dig up the reason why you go about shouting
"Fire!" in crowded theatres. They find it's
because somebody took away your all-day
sucker when you were six.'

'. . . I thought they were called head-
shrinkers.'

'That, I believe, is the medical term.''

(*A Pelican at Blandings*)

. . . or the Outer Hebrides of the Medical profession . . .

I wonder what an osteopath does if a patient
suddenly comes apart in his hands? ('Quick,
Watson, the seccotine!')

(Letter to William Townend, 22 December 1922)

Not that the contemporary Arts exactly came out smelling of roses . . .

If you threw a brick . . . you would be certain to brain some rising young interior decorator, some Vorticist sculptor or a writer of revolutionary *vers libre*. And a very good thing, too.

(*The Small Bachelor*)

In fact, you couldn't trust any of them further than you could throw that brick . . .

Many a man may look respectable, and yet be able to hide at will behind a spiral staircase.

('Success Story' from *Nothing Serious*)

CHAPTER SIX

America,
I Like You

'Hang it!' said Bill to himself in the cab, 'I'll go to America!' The exact words probably which Columbus had used, talking the thing over with his wife.

(*Uneasy Money*)

*

'It looks like New York,' I said to myself as I emerged from the Customs sheds. 'It smells like New York. Yes, I should say it was New York all right.'

*

To say that New York came up to its advance billing would be the baldest of under-statements. Being there was like being in heaven, without going to all the bother and expense of dying.

Why America? I have often wondered about that. Why, I mean, from my earliest years . . . was it America that was always to me the land of romance? It is not as though I had been intoxicated by visions of cowboys and Red Indians. Even as a child I never really became cowboy conscious and to Red Indians I was definitely allergic. I wanted no piece of them.

* * * *

By 1904 Wodehouse had his feet firmly under the table at *The Globe* and was beginning to have his fiction – almost exclusively school stories – published on a regular basis. One of the biggest perks the paper offered its employees was a five-week vacation and now, he determined, was the time to fulfil another of his dreams – to visit America.

'And came a day when I realised that I was sufficiently well fixed to . . . pay a visit to America . . . People would see me walking along with a glassy look in my eyes and my mouth hanging open as if I had adenoids and would whisper to one another, "He's thinking of America." And they were right.' He likened his yearning to that of a Tin Pan Alley songwriter longing 'to get back, back, back to his old Kentucky shack'.

The fare was not excessive, the trip took nine days each way, so he would have a clear fortnight in New York. On 14 April he set sail on the *St Louis* . . .

* * * *

The Captain was on the bridge, pretty sure he knew the way to New York but, just to be on the safe side, murmuring to himself, 'Turn right at Cherbourg and then straight on.'

('Life With Freddie' from *Plum Pie*)

He set to work swiftly and silently, like a New York Customs official dealing with the effects of a star of the musical comedy stage who has left her native America for a trip to Paris and, returning, has announced that she has nothing to declare.

(*Money in the Bank*)

* * * *

He found a different world with different manners. There was the little matter of getting a drink. When he arrived in 1921, for instance, Prohibition was in force . . .

Our first act was to summon a bell-boy and give him the Sinister Whisper, to which he replied with a conspiratorial nod and buzzed off, returning later with a bottle of whisky — at the nominal price of $17!!! I suppose if you tried to get champagne here, you'd have to throw in your Sunday trousers as well.

Apparently you can still get the stuff, but you have to be darned rich.

(Letter to Leonora Wodehouse, 2 April 1921)

* * * *

The squarest man, deposited suddenly in New York and faced with the prospect of earning his living there is likely to quail for a moment. New York is not like other cities. London greets the stranger with a sleepy grunt. Paris giggles. New York howls.

(*The Prince and Betty*)

*

There are several million inhabitants of New York. Not all of them eke out a precarious livelihood by murdering one another . . .

(Introduction to *Psmith Journalist*)

*

On a typical sweltering late August afternoon one might well find '[one half of the populace] crawling about asking those they met if this was hot enough for them, the

other maintaining that what they minded was
not so much the heat as the humidity.

(*Sam the Sudden*)

*

In 1904 I found residents in the home of the
brave and the land of the free, though
delightful chaps if you got to know them,
rather on the brusque side. They shoved you
in the street and asked you who you were
shoving, and used, when spoken to, only one
side of the mouth in replying. They were, in
a word, pretty tough eggs.

Fifty years later, however, he found 'its inhabitants as polite as
pallbearers . . . perhaps it is because I have been over here
setting a good example'.

Conversation on the New York Subway is
impossible. The ingenious gentlemen who
constructed it started with the object of
making it noisy. Not ordinary noisy like a ton
of coal falling onto a sheet of tin, but really
noisy. So they fashioned the pillars of thin
steel, and the sleepers of thin wood, and
loosened all the nuts, and now a Subway train

in motion suggests a prolonged dynamite explosion blended with the voice of some great cataract.

(*Psmith, Journalist*)

To see the Subway in its most characteristic mood one must travel on it during the rush hour, when its patrons are packed into the carriages in one solid jam by muscular guards and policemen, shoving in a manner reminiscent of a Rugby football scrum.

(*Psmith, Journalist*)

I took to American food from the start like a starving Eskimo flinging himself on a portion of blubber. The poet Keats, describing his emotions on first reading Chapman's Homer, speaks of himself as feeling like some watcher of the skies when a new planet swims into his ken. Precisely so did I feel . . . when the waiter brought me my first slab of strawberry shortcake . . . 'No matter if it puts an inch on my waistline,' I said to myself, 'I must be in on this.'

And people would try and sell one things – like the Brooklyn Bridge, for example . . .

I don't say I've ever sold Central Park or the Brooklyn Bridge to anybody, but if I can't get rid of a parcel of home-made oil stock to a guy that lives in the country, I'm losing my grip and ought to retire.

(*Money for Nothing*)

. . . they were clearly a species apart . . .

In my experience there are two kinds of elderly American. One, the stout and horn-rimmed, is matiness itself. He greets you as if you were a favourite son, starts agitating the cocktail shaker before you know where you are, slips a couple into you with a merry laugh, claps you on the back, tells you a dialect story about two Irishmen named Pat and Mike, and, in a word, makes life one grand, sweet song. The other, which runs a good deal to the cold, grey stare and the square jaw, seems to view the English cousins with concern. It is not Elfin. It broods. And every now and then you catch its eye, and it is like colliding with a raw oyster.

(*Thank You, Jeeves*)

. . . while the younger generation were clearly obsessed with sex . . .

If the youth of America has a fault, it is that it is always a bit inclined, when something shapely looms up on the skyline, to let its mind wander from the business at hand.

('The Unpleasantness at Kozy Kot' from *A Few Quick Ones* (US edition))

For, like so many substantial Americans, he had married young and kept on marrying, springing from blonde to blonde like the chamois of the Alps leaping from crag to crag.

(*Summer Moonshine*)

[Wilbur Trout] lost all restraint, springing from blonde to blonde with an assiduity which seemed to suggest that he intended to go on marrying them till the supply gave out.

(*A Pelican at Blandings*)

* * * *

Nonetheless, the return fare seemed to Wodehouse a good investment. In his diary he wrote — 'In New York gathering experience. Worth many guineas in the future, but none for the moment.'

After that trip to New York I was a man who counted . . . The manner of editors towards me changed. Whereas before it had been, 'Throw this man out,' they now said, 'Come in, my dear fellow, come in and tell us all about America.'

He was, indeed, prescient, for on his return to England in May, he was able to place numerous pieces imbued with his New Worldly wisdom. August, for instance, found him regaling the readers of *Punch* with 'Society Whispers From The States'.

(Later – in *Carry On, Jeeves* – he would have Lady Malvern drop into Bertie's New York apartment, firmly convinced that a one-month stay was perfectly ample to write her *magnum opus* – *America and the Americans*. After all, a friend of hers had produced *America from Within* after being there only two weeks!)

He also began to sell his work in America and – as a symbol of his new status as an authentic Anglo-American author – he even acquired a US agent, one A. E. Baerman, who sold a novel, *Love Among the Chickens*, for $1,000.

It was Baerman, in fact, who precipitated Wodehouse's second and more significant visit to the US in 1909. He used the simple device of not paying him the money he owed him. Whether Wodehouse ever did get it is not entirely clear but what he did achieve was to set up literary contacts that would stand him in good stead for years to come, and it was not long before he was inventing the concept of the transatlantic 'commute' – not such an expensive proposition when the second-class fare was only £10 each way. Not that he ever claimed it, but Wodehouse was probably the first significant writer to operate with equal success on both sides of the water. Between 1905 and 1916 his work appeared in some twenty US publications.

His constant companion on his travels was the faithful Monarch typewriter he bought with his first American earnings. For twenty-five years or so it travelled in the lap of luxury, becoming somewhat spoiled and temperamental in the process. Eventually, he had to buy a second model, which was forced to donate its parts to repair the beloved original. The day in 1935 the Monarch finally handed in its dinner pail was a black one in the Wodehouse family circle. He turned to a Royal but old habits died hard – 'I don't like these metal things which stick up and hold the paper down, so that you can't get a clear view of what you're writing.'

> (Incidentally . . . have you ever noticed that if you ever strike a wrong letter on the typewriter it always comes out very clear and firm and black, while with the right letters you have to go back and hammer them twice to make them show at all?)
>
> (Letter to Denis Mackail, December 1945)

In 1956 he bowed to the inevitable — an *electric* typewriter. It received a qualified approval: '. . . every now and then for no discoverable reason it prints an extra letter — as in the word "bestg" above. I'll swear I never hit the "g" key. The bally machine simply decided that a "g" would look well at the end of the word "best" and shoved it in.'

With a little help from some of his new literary friends, he managed to sell short stories to *Cosmopolitan* and *Collier's* for $200 and $300 respectively. Such success was heady stuff:

> To seize pen and paper and post my resignation to *The Globe* was with me the work of an instant.

He immediately took a room at the Hotel Earle — later symbolically mis-remembered by Wodehouse as the Duke! — and settled in with his Monarch, 'paper, pencils, envelopes and Bartlett's book of *Familiar Quotations,* that indispensable adjunct to literary success . . . It so happens that I am not very bright and find it hard to think up anything really clever off my own bat, but give me my Bartlett and I will slay you.'

I was handicapped as a writer by the fact that I knew nothing about anything. All the other members of my circle had backgrounds on which they could draw . . . I alone had nothing to write about except what I could dig out of a brain which had never amounted to much at the best of times . . . I had a certain facility for dialogue and a nice light comedy touch – at least, I thought it was nice – but what I needed was plots . . . Plots were my trouble.

After a while he found that 'I had become a slanter.'

A slanter is a writer who studies what editors want. He reads the magazines carefully and turns out stories as like the ones they are publishing as he can manage without actual plagiarism. It is a deadly practice.

(Introduction to *The Man with Two Left Feet*)

The hotel was in the heart of bohemian Greenwich Village. In the musical, *Oh, Lady! Lady!!* (1918) he would immortalise it in song:

Oh, down in Greenwich Village
There's something, 't would appear,
Demoralizing in the atmosphere.
Quite ordinary people
Who come and live down here
Get changed to perfect nuts within a year.
It's a sort of kind of something in the air . . .

My favourite Aunt Matilda
Found Oshkosh rather slow,
So she moved to Greenwich Village
And took a studio
When she was eighty-three years old or so.
She learned the ukulele,
She breakfasted at Polly's,
And, what is worse,
She wrote free verse,
And now she's in the Follies!

I was very hard up in my Greenwich Village days, but I was always very happy. There were trees and grass and, if you wanted to celebrate the sale of a story, two wonderful old restaurants, the Brevoort and the Lafayette . . . everything such as food and hotel bills was inexpensive: one could live on

practically nothing, which was fortunate for
me because I had to.

(Introduction to *The Small Bachelor*)

* * * *

Like Shakespeare's *Tempest*, the Isle of Manhattan was full of
noises — not merely the traffic that Wodehouse had complained
about but the sound of the various accents that made up its
ethnic melting pot. For a writer with Wodehouse's ear it was a
mother lode and before long he was weaving the speech
patterns of the city streets into his dialogue. J. B. Priestley was
to claim that, if this wasn't the way American gangsters talked,
it was certainly the way 'they would like to talk'.

By contrast with his native woodnotes wild, he found
American English to be a zestful living language and he
contributed several coinages of his own. The *Oxford Dictionary*
credits him with introducing such words and phrases as — 'To
put on the dog', 'to give someone the elbow', 'lulu',
'hoosegow', 'hornswoggle', 'calaboose', 'lallapaloosa', 'crust'
(for nerve) and 'to oil out'. There are probably many more for
the lexicographer to disinter.

In Wodehouse's hands it added up to a unique literary *argot*.

When two countries are divided by a common language,
there are bound to be times when confusions occur. One such
happened to Ethel Wodehouse — much to her husband's
amusement:

Did Mummie tell you about herself at the
highbrow dinner in New York? Somebody
asked her what she thought about the League

of Nations, and she said it was a wonderful production but lacking in comedy and that the dresses were wonderful. Thinking they were talking about *The League of Notions.* Droll, what?

(Letter to Leonora Wodehouse – 1 May 1921)

* * * *

Like so many of its visitors, he found New York to be a cornucopia in so many ways . . .

In New York you may find every class of paper which the imagination can conceive . . . If an Esquimau came to New York, the first thing he would find on the bookstalls in all probability would be the *Blubber Magazine,* or some similar production written by Esquimaux for Esquimaux. Everybody reads in New York and reads all the time.

(*Psmith, Journalist*)

. . . though later in life he was to become less enthusiastic about the content of what he read . . .

American papers today go in exclusively for gloom . . . The only ones that do not prophesy the collapse of civilisation at 3.30

sharp (Eastern Standard Time) a week from Wednesday are those who make it Tuesday afternoon at 2.45.

In those early days, however, it was the multitude of magazines that kept him going. Most of his income was coming from the pulp magazines . . . 'There was practically one per person . . . and it was entirely owing to them that I was able in those days to obtain the calories without which it is fruitless to try and keep the roses in the cheeks.'

Later he would come to realise why he was not having comparable success with the prestige magazines – his *name* was all wrong:

My pulp magazine stories had been by 'P. G. Wodehouse' . . . and this at a time when a writer in America who went about without three names was practically going around naked . . . Those were the days of . . . Earl Derr Biggers . . . Mary Roberts Rinehart, Clarence Buddington Kelland . . . And here was I, poor misguided simp, trying to get by with a couple of contemptible initials . . . In anything like a decent magazine I would have stood out as conspicuously as a man in a sweater and cap at the Eton and Harrow match.

For some time to come his byline would now read – 'Pelham Grenville Wodehouse' – and it seemed to do the trick. Only when he received $20,000 for a serial in the *Saturday Evening Post* did he feel 'safe in becoming P. G. Wodehouse again'.

* * * *

As a pioneer commuter Wodehouse eventually found himself facing a problem that was to dog him for years – income tax.

The general problem about the income-tax appears to have been that it is all right this time, but it mustn't happen again. I was looking through a volume of *Punch* for the year 1882 the other day, and I came across a picture of a gloomy-looking individual paying his tax.

'I can just do it this time', he is saying, 'but I wish you would tell Her Majesty that she mustn't look on me as a source of income in the future.'

At first I felt toward the United States Government as I would feel towards any perfect stranger who insinuated himself into my home and stood me on my head and went through my pockets. The only difference I could see between the United States

Government and the ordinary practitioner in a black mask was that the latter usually left his victim carfare.

(*Vanity Fair*, May 1919)

In fact, it turned out to be twin problems. International tax law had yet to recognise the possibility of transatlantic travel – with the result that he found himself being taxed on his income from the UK and the US by *both* countries.

I'm off tomorrow to Paris . . . I find that if I stay longer than six months [in England] I am liable to pay income tax on everything I make in America as well as England, in addition to paying American income tax!

(Letter to William Townend – 11 February 1921))

Over the years various advisors offered him a number of imaginative suggestions to circumvent this archaic legislation, while remaining within the law. Some worked, some didn't and all were expensive. In a situation worthy of a Wodehouse plot, several were taken to court by the revenue authorities as test cases.

In the UK Wodehouse prevailed against the Special Commissioners but the US situation turned out to be more complex. However, he managed to win his fair share of the legal arguments and even appeared successfully before the Supreme Court at the end of the 1940s before the Great Tax Saga ended.

It was a subject which was to recur both in his fiction and his private correspondence . . .

In his dedication to *Right Ho, Jeeves* (1935) he originally intended to make a flamboyant dedication to Raymond Needham, KC, the man who had represented him before the Special Commissioners . . .

> Who put the tax-gatherers to flight
> When they had their feet on my neck
> And their hands on my wallet.

. . . but was eventually persuaded that he might further antagonise the Inland Revenue and so restricted himself to a more orthodox line!

> '[Uncle Tom's] just had a demand from the income tax people for fifty-eight pounds one and threepence, and all he's been talking about since I got back has been ruin and the sinister trend of socialistic legislation and what will become of us all.
>
> (*Right Ho, Jeeves*)

*

> 'Why dash it, if I could think of some way of doing down the income-tax people, I should be a rich man. You don't know a way of doing down the income-tax people, do you Bertie?'

'Sorry, no. I doubt if even Jeeves does.'
(*The Mating Season*)

*

When government assessors call
To try and sneak your little all
You simply hit them with an axe;
It's how you pay your income tax
In Bongo, it's on the Congo
And I wish that I was there.
('Bongo on the Congo' from *Sitting Pretty*)

* * * *

New York never ceased to fascinate, warts and all. When he returned after the war for what was to be a permanent stay, he told a radio interviewer – 'Every time I come back to New York it is like meeting an old sweetheart and finding she has put on a lot of weight.'

And radio had created another cultural phenomenon . . .

Except for the occasional gruff grunter, all New York taxi drivers are rapid-fire comedians, and they are given unlimited scope for their Bob Hopefulness by the fact that in American cabs there is no glass shutter separating them from their customer . . . If

you take a taxi nowadays, your ride is not so
much a ride as an audition.

But New York was to provide Wodehouse with the ultimate
revelation . . .

In New York, I have always found, one gets
off the mark quickly in matters of the heart.
This, I believe, is due to something in the air.
(Thank You, Jeeves)

In the Big Apple Plum was to find his Eve. Pelham Grenville
Wodehouse fell in love . . .

CHAPTER SEVEN

Pearls, Girls . . . and Plums

A successful marriage is not so much to do with
whether a couple is in love as a shared communion
of tastes that enable them to live with each other
harmoniously.

> (Letter to Leslie H. Bradshaw – 24 October 1914)

I began to realise that my ideal wife was something
. . . a lot more clinging and drooping and prattling,
and what not.

> (Bertie in 'Jeeves Takes Charge' from *Carry On, Jeeves*)

'What was it the poet said of couples like the Bingese?'

'"Two minds with but a single thought, two hearts that beat as one", sir.'

'A dashed good description, Jeeves.'

'It has, I believe, given universal satisfaction, sir.'

('Jeeves and the Old School Chum' from *Very Good, Jeeves*)

All you need is a girl,
Just one dear little girl
Standing near to cheer you
When everything seems going wrong.
Though the going is tough,
You'll win through sure enough:
All you need to succeed
Is a girl just to help you along.
('All You Need Is A Girl' – *Sitting Pretty*)

* * * *

On 3 August 1914 Wodehouse found himself making up the fourth on a blind date – though it's doubtful that he realised what it was called or that he was on one. He had arrived in New York only the day before and the occasion was certainly propitious in more ways than one. It was the day World War I broke out . . .

Before he left England he had tried to enlist but, once again, his eyesight was the decisive factor – 'I was rejected for service because of my eyes. They had been bad as a child and I was kept out of the navy because of them. I tried to enlist again over here [the US] when America went to war, but I was rejected once more.'

Ethel Rowley Wayman (*née* Newton) was a widow and four years younger than Wodehouse. She was the precise opposite of him in almost every way – vivacious and worldly where he was shy and almost antisocial. They were clearly meant to be two sides of one coin and within days Wodehouse had proposed to her.

Their courtship was informal, to say the least. Every day Wodehouse would take his intended bathing at Long Beach, Long Island. 'We used to go down to the Pennsylvania Railroad Station. We'd ride down to Long Beach and have a swim and lunch, and then come back on the train. Of course, there were hardly any motors then. Anyway, I couldn't have afforded that.'

On 30 September they were married at the Little Church Around the Corner on East 29th Street at Madison Avenue.

Wodehouse was to write a song about it that was used in *Sally* (1920):

> *Dear little Church 'Round the Corner,*
> *Where so many lives have begun,*
> *Where folks without money see nothing that's*
>   *funny*
> *In two living cheaper than one.*
> *Our hearts to each other we've trusted:*
> *We're busted, but what do we care?*
> *For a moderate price*

> *You can start dodging rice*
> *At the Church 'Round the Corner,*
> *It's just 'round the corner,*
> *The corner of Madison Square.*

For the next sixty-one years Ethel was to stand as a shield between him and the rest of the world, except where his writing was concerned. One can't speak for her but for him it was an ideal marriage. 'It was an awfully curious thing how everything altered just after we got married.'

> Married life really is the greatest institution that ever was. When I look back and think of the rotten time I have been having all my life, compared with this, it makes me sick.
>
> (Letter to Leslie Bradshaw, 10 October 1914)

He might even have offered Ethel the advice he put into the mouth of a character in *The Adventures of Sally* 1922:

> Chumps always make the best husbands. When you marry, Sally, grab a chump. Tap his forehead first, and if it rings solid, don't hesitate. All the unhappy marriages come from the husbands having brains. What good are brains to a man? They only unsettle him.

It was a role he chose to play in public from then on — and it takes a man with brains to do that!

* * * *

All Wodehouse's biographers seem agreed that he was inhibited emotionally and that this is the reason that there is so little sexuality in his writing. There is quite likely a good deal of truth in that but there may also be a clue in a remark he made to a *Sunday Telegraph* interviewer in 1961 – 'I'm all for incest and tortured souls in moderation, but a good laugh from time to time never hurt anybody.'

Souls in torment and ripped bodices simply didn't fit into the ironically cheerful universe he went to such pains to create out of whole cloth. Love and marriage were all very well – except for Bertie, who must escape the latter at all costs – ('I don't know anything that braces one up like finding you haven't got to get married after all.' – *Jeeves in the Offing*). That apart, they were essentially the stuff of farce for as long as the plot lasted.

* * * *

When it comes to love, there's a lot to be said for the *à la carte* as opposed to the *table d'hôte*.
(*Ring for Jeeves*)

*

Ginger and Magnolia were locked in an embrace so close that it seemed to me that only powerful machinery could unglue them.
(*Much Obliged, Jeeves*)

*

A frightful, tender, melting look, that went through me like a red-hot brad-awl through a pat of butter and filled me with a nameless fear.

(*Joy in the Morning*)

*

A woman's smile is like a bath-tap. Turn it on and you find yourself in hot water.

(*Candlelight*)

*

When I see that profile of hers I feel the only thing worth doing in the world is to grab her and start shouting for clergy and bridesmaids to come running.

('Life with Freddie' from *Plum Pie*)

*

Where one goes wrong when looking for the ideal girl is in making one's selection before walking the full length of the counter.

(*Much Obliged, Jeeves*)

So romantic love – in Wodehouse's fiction – is, at best, dangerously disruptive to the natural male order of things. And at worst . . .

'But what is the love life of newts, if you boil it right down? Didn't you once tell me that they just wagged their tails at one another in the mating season?'

'Quite correct.'

I shrugged my shoulders.

'Well, all right, if they like it. But it's not my idea of molten passion.'

(*The Code of the Woosters*)

*

'Did yer know . . . that the Herring Gull, when it mates, swells its neck, opens its beak and regurgitates a large quantity of undigested food?'

'You don't say? That isn't a part of the Church of England marriage service, is it?'

(*Something Fishy*)

* * * *

Nor would any feminist (without a keen sense of humour) be handing out awards to Wodehouse for his depiction of her sex.

He was in total agreement with Tennyson's description in 'Princess' that woman was like unto 'A rosebud set with little willful thorns!'

So many Wodehouse women had an irritating laugh . . . or, as Jeeves might well have said with Catullus — *Nam risu inepto res ineptior nulla est* ('For there is nothing sillier than a silly laugh').

'She had a penetrating sort of laugh. Rather like a train going into a tunnel.' ('The Pride of the Woosters is Wounded' from *The Inimitable Jeeves*). Honoria Glossop's was 'the sound of the Scotch Express going under a bridge.' ('Jeeves and the Greasy Bird' from *Plum Pie*) . . . 'a lion-tamer making an authoritative announcement to one of the troupe' . . . 'like a squadron of cavalry charging over a tin bridge' ('The Rummy Affair of Old Biffy' from *Carry On, Jeeves*). Or 'waves breaking on a stern and rockbound coast' . . . while Madeline Bassett — 'one of those soppy girls, riddled from head to foot with whimsy' — 'laughed the tinkling, silvery laugh that had got her so disliked by the better element.' (*The Code of the Woosters*). Though, to be fair, if one is in love with the girl, a silvery laugh can also evoke 'the sound ice makes in a jug of beer on a hot day in August' (*The Girl in Blue*).

And Wodehouse women were inclined to be high minded . . .

> Florence Craye was a girl with a wonderful profile, but steeped to the gills in serious purpose.
>
> ('Jeeves Takes Charge' from *Carry On, Jeeves*)

. . . and, of course, by definition, they were all totally illogical . . .

'Is it quite hopeless to reason with you?'
    'Quite. I'm a blonde.'
        (*Baa, Baa, Black Sheep*)

*

'Could you tell me the correct time?'
    'Precisely eleven.'
    'Coo!' said the girl. 'I must hurry, or I shall be late. I'm meeting a gentleman friend on the pier at half-past ten.'
        ('Bramley is So Bracing' from *Nothing Serious*)

*

Veronica . . . is just a sweet simple English girl with about as much brain as would make a jay bird fly crooked, and that's the way I want her!
    (*Galahad at Blandings*)

*

Nature had not given her more than about as much brain as would fit comfortably into an asprin bottle, feeling no doubt that it was better not to overdo the thing . . .
    (*Galahad at Blandings*)

. . . quite likely whimsical . . .

She was definitely the sort of girl who puts her hand over her husband's eyes, as he is crawling into breakfast with a morning head, and says: 'Guess who?'

(*The Code of the Woosters*)

. . . unrealistically romantic . . .

Betty was one of those ardent, vivid girls, with an intense capacity for hero-worship, and I would have supposed that something more in the nature of a plumed knight or a corsair of the deep would have been her ideal. But, of course, if there is a branch of modern industry where the demand is greater than the supply, it is the manufacture of knights and corsairs; and nowadays a girl, however flaming her aspirations, has to take the best she can get.

('A Mixed Threesome' from '*The Clicking of Cuthbert*')

. . . not to mention devious . . .

He had studied Woman, and he knew that when Woman gets into a tight place her first act is to shovel the blame off onto the nearest male.

('Trouble Down at Tudsleigh' from *Young Men in Spats*)

*

The male sex is divided into rabbits and non-rabbits and the female sex into dashers and doormice.

(*Jeeves in the Offing*)

*

She made one of those foolish remarks which do so much to confirm a man in his conviction that women as a sex should be suppressed.

(*Joy in the Morning*)

But perhaps the most damning verdict comes from that serial *fiancé*, Bertie Wooster:

The more a thoughtful man has to do with women, the more extraordinary it seems to him that such a sex should be allowed to clutter the earth. Women, the way I looked at it, simply wouldn't do . . . What a crew! What a crew! I mean to say, what a *crew*! . . .

I think that there ought to be a law, something has got to be done about this sex, or the whole fabric of society will collapse, and then what silly asses we shall all look.

The whole fact of the matter is that all this modern emancipation of women has resulted in them getting it up their noses and not giving a damn what they do. It was not like this in Queen Victoria's day. The Prince Consort would have had a word to say . . .

(*The Code of the Woosters*)

*

Women may be ministering angels when pain and anguish wring the brow: but if at times she sees a chance to prod the loved one and watch him squirm, she hates to miss it.

(*The Small Bachelor*)

*

I've said it before and I'll say it again – girls are rummy. Old Pop Kipling never said a truer word than when he made that crack about the f. of the s. being d. than the m.

(*Right Ho, Jeeves*)

All in all, this love business was overrated . . .

'Love is a wonderful thing.'

Mr Todhunter's ample mouth curled sardonically.

'When you've seen as much of life as I have,' he replied, 'you'd rather have a cup of tea.'

(*Sam the Sudden*)

. . . and as for marriage . . .

'I nearly married for love when I was young and foolish, but I came out of the ether in time.'

(*The Girl in Blue*)

*

Warm though the morning was, he shivered, as only a confirmed bachelor gazing into the naked face of matrimony can shiver.

(*The Old Reliable*)

*

> 'Marriage is not a process for prolonging the life of love, sir, it merely mummifies the corpse.'
>
> (*The Small Bachelor*)

All this and much more in the same vein in the fiction, where the conventions of the printed page allow the reader to stand back and appreciate the individual lines being placed one on top of the other.

But it must be remembered that throughout the early part of his career, at least, he was operating in parallel in other very different conventions – those of the straight play and the musical comedy.

On the stage, for instance, effects had to be much broader. The almost 'musical' construction of much of Wodehouse's prose – and his imagery in particular – would not translate. His work (to use a favourite Wodehouse word) would have to be a good deal more 'raw'. Writing to Guy Bolton in 1939 he says – 'I believe that if we could work up a reasonably dirty Jeeves story, [producer] George Abbott would do it . . . but a Jeeves plot that is all right for a novel isn't rough enough for the New York stage.'

Which meant that the dialogue had to be 'rougher' and more cynical, too . . .

> 'My motto is "Love and Let Love" – with the one stipulation that people who love in glass-houses should breathe on the windows.'
>
> (Monica in *Come On, Jeeves*)

*

'Love is like life insurance. The older you are when you start it, the more it costs.'

(Daniel in *Don't Listen, Ladies*)

*

'Some men decorate their home with old masters and others with old mistresses.'

(Michael in *Don't Listen, Ladies*)

*

'I'm going to pay you the rarest compliment a woman can pay a man. I'm going to tell you the truth.'

(Lady Maud in the play, *A Damsel in Distress*)

*

DR SALLY: Now tell me about your sex-life.

BILL: Well, naturally, I have had experiences, like other men. I admit it. There have been women in my life.

DR SALLY: (*at stethoscope*) Say 'Ninety-nine'.

BILL: Not half as many as that!

(*Good Morning, Bill*)

The world of musical comedy was more romantic and Wodehouse was equally capable of turning on the charm. In *Oh, Boy!* (1917) George and Lou Ellen wonder what might have been, had they met earlier. In a song called 'I Never Knew About You'. George sings:

> *Life might have been Heaven,*
> *If I, then aged seven,*
> *Had met you when you were three.*
> *We'd have made mud pies like affinities,*
> *We'd have known what rapture may be.*
> *I'd have let you feed my rabbit*
> *Till the thing became a habit, dear!*
> *But I never knew about you*
> *And you never knew about me.*

to which Lou Ellen replies:

> *I was often kissed ''neath the mistletoe'*
> *By small boys excited with tea.*

If I'd known that you existed,
I'd have scratched them and resisted, dear,
But I never knew about you
And you never knew about me.

Wodehouse was most at home when he was talking in simple, colloquial language about the way ordinary people felt in their ordinary, realisable lives. So the man of a girl's dreams probably won't ride up on a white charger and carry her off – but the boy next door may steal her heart anyway.

In 'What I'm Longing to Say' from *Leave it to Jane* (1917):

Somehow, whenever I'm with you I never
Can say what I'm longing to say.
When it's too late and you're not near me,
I can find words, but you're not there to hear me.
That's why, when we are together
I just talk of the weather,
Simply because,
When I'm with you, I never
Can say what I'm longing to say.

. . . or in 'A Pal Like You' from *Oh, Boy!*:

Dozens and dozens of girls I have met,
Sisters and cousins of men in my set;
Tried to be cheerful
And give them an earful

Of soft sort of talk, but,
Oh, gosh! the strain — something fearful!
Always found, after a minute or two,
Just to be civil was all I could do.
Now I know why I
Could never be contented.
I was looking for a pal like you.

And in a rare lapse into romantic sincerity — admittedly in an early work — Wodehouse the novelist shows himself perfectly capable of describing the first, fine careless rapture:

Just when the outstanding change had taken place, it would have been beyond him to say. It had come so gradually and imperceptibly, first one feature then another ceasing to offend the eye — here a leg shortening to a decently human length, there a mop of amber hair miraculously tidying itself. He supposed vaguely that it was always this way with girls.

(*Bill the Conqueror*)

* * * *

In his best-known song, 'Bill' — cut from two earlier shows before it stopped the show in the 1927 *Showboat* — Wodehouse makes the ordinary extraordinary, as the heroine sings:

I used to dream that I would discover
The perfect lover
Some day:
I knew I'd recognise him
If ever he came round my way:
I always used to fancy then
He'd be one of the godlike kind of men,
With a giant brain and a noble head
Like the heroes bold
In the books I read.

He's just my Bill,
He has no gifts at all:
A motor car
He cannot steer
And it seems clear
Whenever he dances,
His partner takes chances.
Oh, I can't explain
It's surely not his brain
That makes me thrill.
I love him
Because he's — I don't know —
Because he's just my Bill

* * * *

Of course, one thing all comedy – musical or otherwise – has in common is the romantic conceit so concisely expressed in the Irving Berlin song 'A Man Chases a Girl (Until She Catches Him)' and Wodehouse rang many lyrical changes on it.

For example, the girls in a Wodehouse show were invariably versed in the more traditional feminine wiles. In 'A Little Bit of Ribbon' from *Oh, Boy!* Jane sings:

> *For a little bit of ribbon*
> *And a little bit of lace,*
> *And a little bit of silk that clings,*
> *When together they are linking,*
> *Always sets a fellow winking,*

And they also set him thinking things.
It's a useful combination for
Assisting a flirtation
If you want to get a man beneath your spell,
And although I'm hardly twenty,
I believe I could do plenty —
With a little bit of ribbon,
And a little bit of lace,
And a little bit of silk as well.

Somehow one can't hear Madeline Bassett or Honoria Glossop singing those lyrics.

Nor are the men recognisable from the fiction. With the exception of Bertie, the young men in Wodehouse are pathetically anxious to tie the knot and only the hard hearts of those who hold the purse strings stand in the way. In the show lyrics the situation is usually reversed:

It's a hard, hard world for a man,
For he tries to be wise and remain aloof and chilly,
But along comes something feminine and frilly,
So what's the use?

Though long you've been a gay and giddy bachelor,
There'll come on the scene a girl not like the rest.
You'll notice something in her eye that fills you with
    dismay;

You'll find that when you're with her you can't think
    what to say.
That's a sure, sure sign
You have ceased to be a rover
And your single days are over.
You had best begin rehearsing
For the better-and-the-worsing . . .
        (*Oh, Lady! Lady!!*, 1918)

But women haven't any sense of pity
For, if they had, the bride would stop and think,
She'd say — 'Why should I marry this poor fathead?
What have I got against the wretched gink?'
But no! She fills the church with her relations,
Who would grab him by the coat tails if he ran;
All his pals have been soft-soaped,
And his best man he's been doped.
Women haven't any mercy on a man.
        (*The Girl Behind the Gun*, 1918)

The Hen-Pecked Male as counterbalance to the Mother-in-Law joke.

For some girl's going to come and grab you
Sooner or later! Just wait!
Yes, in a while
With frozen smile

Along the aisle you'll stagger —
That wedding cake will soon be sitting grimly
Upon the plate.
          (*Sitting Pretty, 1924*)

* * * *

If one had to guess, it would seem probable that Wodehouse's remarks on love and marriage are a cocktail that was one part autobiography to nine parts the established comic tradition that provided the 'good laugh'. Certainly, one can hardly see him as the 'rover' whose 'single days are over' but neither would marriage have seemed a threat. Until he met Ethel Rowley it had probably never really crossed his mind as a real life option.

As far as offspring were concerned, fact, again, probably preceded fiction. Babies were most certainly not on the bill of fare — but *children* . , , fully-grown and dribble-free . . . well . . .

'Jeeves, I wish I had a daughter. I wonder what the procedure is.'
    'Marriage is, I believe, considered the preliminary step, sir.'
          ('Bertie Changes His Mind' from *Carry On, Jeeves*)

Marriage had always appalled him, but there was this to be said for it, that married people had daughters.
          (*Jill the Reckless*)

For Wodehouse marriage proved to be both the preliminary and the ultimate step, since in marrying Ethel he acquired as part of the package the ten-year-old step-daughter, Leonora. It was a second case of love at first sight for the confirmed ex-bachelor and within weeks of meeting the girl who become his beloved 'Snorky' he had adopted her.

1ST INTERMISSION

Writing . . . and Writers

From my earliest years I had always wanted to be a writer. I started turning out the stuff at the age of five. (What I was doing before that, I don't remember. Just loafing, I suppose.)

*

I sometimes wonder if I really am a writer. When I look at the sixty-odd books in the shelf with my name on them, and reflect that 10 million of them have been sold, it amazes me that I can have done it. I don't know anything, and I seem incapable of learning . . . I feel I've been fooling the public for fifty years.

(Letter to William Townend, 18 November 1952)

*

Success comes to a writer, as a rule, so gradually that it is always something of a shock to him to look back and realise the heights to which he has climbed.

It was not that I had any particular message for humanity. I am still plugging away and not the ghost of one so far, so it begins to look as though . . . humanity will remain a message short.

* * * *

Just why a writer writes has been debated endlessly and inconclusively. With Wodehouse it was a joyful compulsion. There was simply nothing he ever wanted to do more.

Between 1901 and 1910 his work was published in around forty UK periodicals and – as we have seen – during that time he also began to make inroads into the US market. From 1902 to 1908 he kept a notebook in which he listed his earnings – 'It's very interesting, though I find it slightly depressing, as it shows the depths I used to descend to in order to get the occasional ten-and-six. Gosh, what a lot of slush I wrote! . . . What a curse one's early work is. It keeps popping up.'

Early on – like a lot of other fledgling writers – he slavishly followed J. M. Barrie's advice to write exclusively what editors wanted to publish. 'I avoided the humorous story, which was where my inclinations lay, and went in exclusively for the mushy sentiment which, judging from the magazines, was the thing most likely to bring a sparkle into an editor's eyes. It never worked.' (Later he liked to quote Barrie's contrary dictum – 'that he had made all his money out of smiles, not laughter'.)

My line was good sound English stuff . . . stories of rich girls who wanted to be loved for themselves alone, and escaped convicts breaking into lonely houses on Christmas Eve, when the white snow lay all around . . .

The curious thing about those early days is that, in spite of the blizzard of rejection slips, I had the most complete confidence in myself. I knew I was good. Today [1957] I am a mass of diffidence and I-wonder-if-this-is-going-to-be-all-rightness, and I envy those tough authors, square-jawed and spitting out of the side of their mouths, who are perfectly sure, every time they start a new book, that it will be a masterpiece . . . but with each new book of mine, I have, as I say, always that feeling that this time I have picked a lemon in the garden of literature. A good thing, really, I suppose. Keeps one on one's toes and makes one write every sentence ten times . . . When in due course Charon ferries me across the Styx and everyone is telling everyone else what a rotten writer I was, I hope at least one voice will be heard piping up, 'But he did take trouble.'

* * * *

There was one area, however, in which he could follow both Barrie's advice *and* his own inclinations and that was in the writing of school stories.

In 1898 the *Public School Magazine* was started by publishers A & C Black and a short while later their rivals, Newnes, brought out a competitor in *The Captain*. Both were ready-made for Wodehouse's work. 'Wodehouse Preferred, until then down in the cellar with no takers, began to rise a bit.'

His school stories broke a certain amount of new ground. Much has been made of their lack of sex or religious moralising – the muscular Christianity in which the genre was inclined to indulge – but this is hardly surprising, since these qualities did not reflect their author's personality. Wodehouse's school stories very much did. In them he was able to express the happiness he had known at Dulwich and the personal code by which he and his contemporaries had lived. They were written for himself and his generation of public school-boys – a generation grown older but not altogether grown up – and they rang true.

And there was another component – and one which makes them still readable today. Their style was Early Ironic. While the characters did what they did wholeheartedly, the books' attitude makes it clear to the reader that what we are witnessing is a prelude to real life and not the life itself. Wodehouse the gentle satirist is already at work.

Although the school stories were far from being the sum total of his work in that first decade of the century, they were certainly his most typical and successful. But by the time it ended, other influences were at work and it was time to move on. His final school novel, *Mike* – a combination of two separate serials, *Jackson Junior* and *The Lost Lambs* – was published in 1909, and in November of that year he wrote to a friend, Leslie

Bradshaw that 'The School stories have served their turn, and it would hurt my chances of success to have them bobbing up when I'm trying to do bigger work. I have given up boys' stories absolutely.'

* * * *

Before Charon finally arrived, Wodehouse was to write about a hundred works of fiction (with one partly finished on his hospital bedside table), sixteen plays, eight libretti and lyrics for twenty-eight musical comedies. Asked about his philosophy of writing:

I don't have a set of rules guiding me. I just go on living. You don't notice things when you're writing. Just writing one book after another, that's my life . . . I wrote another book, then I wrote another book, then I wrote another book, and continued to do so down the years . . . But there has never been anything dramatic and sensational about any of my productions. I have always run a quiet, conservative business, just jogging along and endeavouring to give satisfaction [by maintaining quality of output] . . . I would call myself a betwixt-and-between author – not on the one hand a total bust and yet not on the other a wham or socko. Ask the first ten men you meet, 'Have you ever heard of P. G. Wodehouse?' and nine of them will answer, 'No.' The tenth, being hard of hearing, will say, 'Down the passage, first door on the right.'

I am a creature of habit and as a result of forty years of incessant literary composition have become a mere writing machine. Wherever I am, I sit down and write . . . It has all helped to keep me busy and out of the public houses.

How did he get himself started every day?

I sit at my typewriter and curse a bit.

I haven't any violent feelings about anything. I just love writing. What really makes me happy is to get a really good plot for a novel and then sit back and write it.

       (Radio Interview)

I much prefer writing books and short stories to writing dialogue for plays. There's no author's narrative in plays . . .

       (Interview)

Of course, the trouble is that one is never quite happy unless one is working – and by working I don't so much mean the actual writing as the feeling that one could write if one wanted to. It is the in-between times that kill one.

(Letter to William Townend, 13 September 1934)

Throughout his life interviewers rarely managed to elicit a truly serious response from him on the one subject he took extremely seriously. But then, it was not in the Code of the Wodehouses to take oneself seriously in public.

On *why* a writer writes he was a little more forthcoming:

It's a funny thing about writing. If you are a writer by nature, I don't believe you write for money or fame or even for publication, but simply for the pleasure of turning out the stuff . . . What makes a writer write is that he likes writing. Naturally, when he has written something, he wants to get as much for it as he can, but that is a very different thing from writing for money.

* * * *

I don't suppose he makes enough out of a novel to keep a midget in doughnuts for a week. Not a really healthy midget.

(*The Luck of the Bodkins*)

* * * *

In a letter to William Townend written on 5 April 1945, referring to the uninterrupted literary output of his prisoner-of-war years, and at a time when it was uncertain how the British bookbuying public might react:

I really don't care if these books are published or not. The great thing is that I've got them down on paper, and can read and re-read them and polish them and change an adjective for a better one and cut out dead lines.

(In fact, his postwar work proved as popular as ever on both sides of the Atlantic.)

Once the bank was safely behind him, he was never in any doubt as to what his future held:

Certainly I have done much better at writing than I would have done in some of the other professions. I'm thinking at the moment of the second-hand bridge business, snail-gathering and getting hit in the stomach by meteorites . . . As a writer I have always rather kept off snails, feeling that they lacked sustained dramatic interest.

If pressed, he might well have added whelk-stall running to the list . . .

Owing to my having become mentally arrested at an early age, I write the sort of books which people, not knowing the facts, assume to be the work of a cheerful, if backward, young fellow of about twenty-five.

A revealing remark, in many ways, because that was precisely the image he sought to cultivate for the rest of his life.
About the nature of his work he was quite clear:

It's what I always feel about my work — viz. that I go off the rails unless I stay all the time in a sort of artificial world of my own creation. A real character in one of my books sticks out like a sore thumb.

It was all very well for him to say it about his own work but the same remark from a third party would not pass unremarked . . .

George Orwell calls my stuff Edwardian (which God knows it is. No argument about that, George) and says that the reason for it being Edwardian is that I did not set foot in England for sixteen years and so lost touch with conditions there. Sixteen years, mark you, during most of which I was living in London and was known as Beau Wodehouse of Norfolk Street.

You're right about my books being early Edwardian. I look upon myself as an historical novelist . . . I don't believe it matters and intend to go on hewing to the butler line, let the chips fall where they may . . . my stuff has been out of date since 1914 and nobody has seemed to mind.

(Letter to Denis Mackail, December 1945)

His literary ambitions, he claimed, were modest enough:

I feel about my stuff that it never contains what you might call surprises. You are never likely to feel like Keats on first reading Chapman's Homer but I do have the ambition to keep the old Wodehouse pemmican up to the level.

(Letter to Denis Mackail, 12 April 1931)

[*143*]

. . . an endeavour, he tended to feel, not exactly helped by
fellow professionals giving the game away . . .

[J. B. Priestley, for instance] 'analyses me,
blast him, and called attention to the thing I
try and hush up – viz that I have only got one
plot and produce it once a year with variations. I wish to goodness novelists wouldn't
review novels . . .

(Letter to Denis Mackail, October 1932)

In an ideal world a chap would just produce the stuff and leave
it like that. Unfortunately, the writer's world intends to be
littered with gushing readers – as Bertie found when he was
confused with the Barbara Cartlandesque writer, Rosie M.
Banks . . .

'My nephew has probably told you that I have
been making a close study of your books of
late?'

'Yes, he did mention it. How – er – how
did you like the bally things?'

'Mr Wooster, I am not ashamed to say that
the tears came into my eyes as I listened to
them. It amazes me that a man as young as
you can have been able to plumb human
nature so surely to its depth; to play with so

unerring a hand on the quivering heart-strings of your reader; to write novels so true, so human, so moving, so vital!'

'Oh, it's just a knack,' I said.

The good old persp. was bedewing my forehead by this time in a pretty lavish manner. I don't know when I've been so rattled.

('No Wedding Bells for Bingo' from *The Inimitable Jeeves*)

*

Everyone has some pet aversion — some dislike slugs, some cockroaches; George disliked women writers.

('Parted Ways' from *Strand Magazine*, December 1914)

* * * *

She wrote novels: and that instinct of self-preservation which lurks in every publisher had suggested to him that behind her invitation lay a sinister desire to read those to him one by one.

The rich contralto of female novelist calling to its young had broken the stillness of the summer afternoon.

('Mr Potter Takes a Rest Cure' from *Blandings Castle*)

*

The Agee woman told us for three quarters of an hour how she came to write her beastly book, when a simple apology was all that was required.

(*The Girl in Blue*)

* * *

Wodehouse always publicly demurred at the idea of writing an out-and-out autobiography – although he found a cunning oblique way round it in *Over Seventy*, *Performing Flea* and *Bring on the Girls* . . .

The three essentials for an autobiography are that its compiler should have an eccentric father, a miserable misunderstood childhood and a hell of a time at his public school, and I enjoyed none of these advantages. My father was as normal as rice pudding, my childhood went like a breeze from start to finish, with everybody I met understanding me perfectly, while as for my school days at Dulwich, they were just six years of unbroken bliss.

Should he be put on the rack and *made* to write it . . .

I could mention, for instance, that when I was four years old I used to play with an orange, but I doubt that would interest them, and that at the age of six I read the whole of Pope's Iliad

[which we happen to know he did]

which, of course, they wouldn't believe.

And as for adolescence, I recall nothing except that I had a lot of pimples. (Today I have none. How often that happens! We start out in life with more pimples than we know what to do with and, in the careless arrogance of youth, fancy that they are going to last forever; but one morning we find we are down to our last half dozen, and then those go. There is a lesson in this for all of us, I think.) . . . Better, I think, to skip childhood and adolescence . . .

What infernally dull reading an author's life makes. It's all right as long as you are still struggling but once you have become financially sound there is nothing to say.

(Letter to Denis Mackail, 22 July 1955)

* * * *

Wodehouse was a little more forthcoming when it came to discussing his working methods:

I now write short stories at terrific speed. I've started a habit of rushing them through and then working over them very carefully, instead of trying to get the first draft exactly right, and have just finished the rough draft of an 8,000 word story in two days. It nearly slew me. As a rule, I find a week long enough for a short story, if I have the plot well thought out . . . On a novel I generally do eight pages a day – i.e., about 2,500 words . . . As a rule I like to start work in the mornings, knock off for a breather, and then do a bit more before dinner. I never work after dinner . . . Usually when I get to the last fifty pages of a story, it begins to write itself.

Naturally, age took its toll. In a letter to Guy Bolton he laments
the fact:

When I remember that I wrote the last
twenty-six pages of *Thank You, Jeeves* in a
single day, I sigh for the past. Pretty darned
good if I get three done nowadays.

I have never written a novel yet (except
Thank You, Jeeves) without doing 40,000
words or more and finding they were all
wrong and going back and starting again, and
this after filling 400 pages with notes, mostly
delirious, before getting anything in the
nature of a coherent scenario.

Nonetheless, the constant process of revision invariably paid off
for him and when he comes to review the finished article . . .

It really reads as if I had written it straight off
without a pause.

Not that what he read always struck him as his best stuff:

Golly, what rot it sounds when one writes it
down! Come, come, Wodehouse, is *this* the
best you can do in the way of carrying on the

great tradition of English Literature? Still, I'll bet the plot of *Hamlet* seemed just as lousy when Shakespeare was trying to tell it to Ben Jonson in the Mermaid Tavern. ('Well, Ben, see what I mean, the central character is this guy, see, who's in love with this girl, see, but her old man doesn't think he's on the level, see, so he tells her — wait a minute, I better start at the beginning. Well, so this guy's in college, see, and he's come home because his mother's gone and married his uncle, see, and he sees a ghost, see. So this ghost turns out to be the guy's father . . .')

(Letter to William Townend, 23 April 1932)

I sometimes wish I wrote that powerful stuff the reviewers like so much, all about incest and homosexualism.

(Letter to Denis Mackail, 28 February 1960)

On the other hand, enough of this self-flagellation . . .

I wonder why people feel that writing dull books about, say, Shakespeare's humour is respectable, but writing funny books themselves is *infra dig*?

Writer's bloc is a recurrent theme:

> After three months' absolute deadness my
> brain begins to whir like a dynamo . . . I
> believe our rotten brains have to go through
> these ghastly periods of inertness before
> getting second wind . . . But if a writer keeps
> on writing, something generally breaks
> eventually.

. . . although, in reality, it was never a serious problem for him
and even a diminished Wodehouse output would have seemed
ambitious for most 'serious' writers. Even someone as
dedicated as Graham Greene would talk of his daily 350 words.
Of those whose methods have been recorded only Anthony
Trollope seems to have come close. He claimed to finish one
novel and start immediately on the next. Wodehouse was more
than a little intrigued . . .

> Did he sit down each morning and write
> exactly 1,500 words, without knowing when
> he sat down how the story was going to
> develop, or had he a careful scenario on
> paper? . . . Of course, if he did plan the
> whole thing out first, there is nothing so very
> bizarre in the idea of writing so many
> hundred words of it each day. After all, it is
> more or less what one does oneself. One sits

down to work each morning, no matter whether one feels bright or lethargic, and before one gets up a certain amount of stuff, generally about 1,500 words, has emerged. But to sit down before a blank sheet of paper without an idea of how the story is to proceed and just start writing seems to me impossible.

(Letter to William Townend, 30 June 1945)

He flirted briefly with the idea of dictating his material:

How can anybody dictate? I should be feeling shy and apologetic all the time. The nearest I ever got was when Ethel brought me one of those machines Edgar Wallace used to use, where you talk on to a wax cylinder . . . when I played it back, I was appalled how unfunny the stuff sounded. I hadn't known it till then but apparently I have a voice like a very pompous clergyman intoning. Either that or the instrument was pulling my leg. Anyway, I sold the damn thing next day.

(Letter to William Townend, 13 September 1945)

As far as the 'stuff' itself was concerned . . . he wrote to Townend, a fellow writer:

I suppose the secret of writing is to go through your stuff until you come on something you think is particularly good, and then cut it out.

(Letter to William Townend, November 1923)

I believe over-longness is the worst fault in writing . . . Isn't it odd how one can spoil a story by being too leisurely in telling it?

. . . and in a later (29 April 1946) letter he would ally himself with Kipling, who maintained that 'the principal thing in writing is to cut . . . it's like raking slag out of a fire to make the fire burn brighter. I know just what he means . . . The trouble is to know what to cut. I generally find with my own stuff that it's unnecessary lines in the dialogue that are wrong, but then my books are principally dialogue.'

I write primarily to have something to read in the long winter evenings, and the heart of England is still sound . . .

Before he got into his stride as a writer of full-length novels Wodehouse was heavily involved in writing for the musical theatre. ('Simultaneously short stories and musical comedies kept fluttering out of me like bats out of a barn.') It was to influence his sense of construction and pace ever afterwards:

I believe there are two ways of writing novels. One of them is mine, making the thing a sort of musical comedy without music, and ignoring real life altogether; the other is going right deep down into life and not caring a damn. The ones that fail are the ones where the writer loses his nerve and says, 'My God! I can't write this, I must tone it down.'

(Letter to William Townend, 23 January 1935)

The more I write the more I am convinced that the only way to write a popular story is to split it up into scenes, and have as little stuff between the scenes as possible. The principle I always go on in writing a long story is to think of the characters as if they were living salaried actors. The one thing actors — important actors, I mean — won't stand is being brought on to play a scene which is of no value to them in order that they may feed some less important character, and I believe this isn't vanity but is based on an instinctive knowledge of stagecraft . . .

(Letter to William Townend)

Writing the dialogue for them to say was never a problem from the first. But what did they *look* like?

I find the most difficult thing in writing is to describe a character. Appearance, I mean.

(Letter to William Townend, 15 May 1938)

What a sweat a novel is till you are sure of your characters. And what a vital thing it is to have plenty of things for a major character to *do*. That is the test. If they aren't in situations, characters can't be major characters, not even if you have the rest of the troupe talk their heads off about them.

(Letter to William Townend)

People are always asking me . . . well, someone did the other day . . . if I draw my characters from living figures. I don't. I never have, except in the case of Psmith. He was based more or less faithfully on Rupert D'Oyly Carte, son of the Savoy theatre man. He was at school with a cousin of mine, and my cousin happened to tell me about his monocle, his immaculate clothes and his habit, when asked by a master how he was, of replying: 'Sir, I grow thinnah and thinnah.' I instantly realised that I had been handed a piece of cake and bunged him down on paper, *circa* 1908.

The 'P' in Psmith, of course, was silent ('as in pshrimp'). 'Like the tomb. Compare such words as ptarmigan, psalm, and phthisis.'

The other exception Wodehouse might have made is Stanley Featherstonehaugh Ukridge, who appears to have been based on a friend of his young days called Herbert Westbrook, seasoned with a hint or two of his old school chum and lifetime correspondent, William Townend. Thereafter, everyone else was a hybrid.

He was well aware of the ingredients he required:

I have to have jewels, comic lovers and about a dozen American crooks before I can move.

. . . and where his orientation lay. He was a humorist, pure but never simple . . .

Humorists, as I see it, have always been looked askance at, if not actually viewed with concern. At English schools in my boyhood they were divided into two classes, both unpopular. If you merely talked amusingly, you were a 'silly ass' ('You *are* a silly ass!' was the formula). If your conversation took a mordant and satirical turn, you were a 'funny swine'. And whichever you were, you were scorned and despised and lucky not to get kicked. It is to this early discouragement that I attribute the fact that no Englishman, grown to man's estate, ever says anything brighter than 'Eh, what?' and 'Most extraordinary.'

In order to be a humorist, you must see the world out of focus, and today, when the world is really out of focus, people insist that you see it straight. Humour implies ridicule of the established institutions, and they want to keep their faith in the established order intact.

(*Over Seventy*)

If as you walk along the streets of any city [in America] you see a furtive-looking man who slinks past you like a cat in a strange alley which is momentarily expecting to receive a half-brick in the short ribs, don't be misled into thinking it is Baby Face Schultz, the racketeer for whom the police of thirty states are spreading a dragnet. He is probably a humorist.

In later years he sometimes found new styles of humour a little disconcerting. Reviewing *The Best of Punch 1957* he confessed that 'the difference between wit and humour has always beaten me'. At least half the pieces in the collection, he considered, 'will give grave offence to somebody or other. For everything humorous (or witty) does give offence nowadays.'

* * * *

He had a domelike head, piercing eyes, and that cynical twist of the upper lip which generally means an epigram on the way.

(*America, I Like You*)

* * * *

But except for those first Barrie-influenced years, Wodehouse stuck to what he instinctively knew he could do and created his cockeyed, timeless universe. And – lo and behold! – the editors found they wanted to publish it and went on wanting to for decades. When in 1953 Penguin reprinted five titles in one day, putting a million Wodehouses into print, they put him on a new and higher plateau – a Mount Olympus of publishing.

Not that the lower slopes had been exactly unimpressive. As early as the 1920s his name was beginning to be a literary *nonpareil* – not to say a *sine qua non*, dash it!

As a matter of fact, I really am becoming rather a blood these days. In a review of *Wedding Bells* at the Playhouse the critic says 'So-and-so is good as a sort of P. G. Wodehouse character.' And in a review of a book in *The Times* they say 'The author at times reverts to the P. G. Wodehouse manner' . . .

This, I need scarcely point out to you, is jolly old fame. Once they begin to refer to you in that casual way as if everybody must know who you are, all is well.

(Letter to Leonora Wodehouse, 7 August 1920)

. . . and later:

. . . a letter turned up the other day addressed to 'P. G. Wodehouse, London'. I am going to write to myself and address it 'P. G. Wodehouse, England', and see if it arrives. The next step will be to send one addressed simply 'P. G. Wodehouse'.

(Letter to Leonora Wodehouse, 12 September 1924)

The only real problem he ever had in those early days was establishing himself in America. One editor asked him to write stories 'about American characters in an American setting' – which caused Wodehouse to fume:

It can't have come on him as a stunning shock to find that I was laying my scene in England. What did he expect from me? . . . I'm all for spreading a little happiness as I go by, so I told him I would have a pop at some Hollywood stories.

If only those blighters would realise that I started writing about Bertie Wooster and comic earls because I was in America and couldn't write American stories and the only English characters the American public would read about were exaggerated dudes. It's as simple as that. Another thing I object to in these analyses of one's work is that the writer picks out something one wrote in 1907 to illustrate some tendency. Good Lord! I was barely articulate in 1907!

(Letter to Denis Mackail, 1951)

He was to come across one other irritation – the tendency of publishers to want to retitle his books . . .

The Editor of the *Newnes* magazine which is running *Sam in the Suburbs* serially wants to change the title and has decided on *SUNSHINE SAM!!!!* I have written him an anguished letter of protest.

Can you imagine such a foul title? Isn't it pure Ruby M. Ayres? The only thing it could be except Ruby M. Ayres is Harold Bell Wright, in which case Sunshine Sam would be a quaint, drawling old westerner, who cheers up the other cowboys with his homely philosophy, showing that you can be happy though poor, provided you do as the good book says.

(Letter to Leonora Wodehouse, 30 March 1925)

Other than that, Wodehouse suffered most of the other minor problems an author is heir to.

There were the Critics . . .

Why is it that a single slam from even the most patent imbecile can undo all the praise of a hundred critics?
(Letter to Denis Mackail)

I could see by the way she sniffed that she was about to become critical. There has always been a strong strain of book-reviewer blood in her.
(*Aunts Aren't Gentlemen*)

Has anyone ever seen a dramatic critic in the daytime? Of course not. They come out after dark, up to no good.

. . . the Life Sedentary . . .

If I go for an exercise walk, I'm too tired to write, and if I don't get any exercise, my brain doesn't work!

. . . the Adoring Public . . .

When I write a book, the golden words come pouring out like syrup, but let a smiling woman steal up to me with my latest and ask me to dash off something clever on the front page, and it is as though some hidden hand had removed my brain and substituted for it an order of cauliflower.

He took to writing –

> *You like my little stories, do ya?*
> *Oh, glory, glory, hallelujah!*

('It sometimes goes well, sometimes not.')

Although he did his best to keep his admirers at a safe distance, there were social occasions that could not be avoided. On one of them, unbeknownst to him, 'Fate was quietly slipping the lead into the boxing-glove' (*Very Good, Jeeves*). All evening long at a Hollywood dinner the lady sitting next to him rhapsodised over his work. Her sons, she gushed, had masses of his books and never missed reading each new one as it came out. 'And when I tell them that I have actually been sitting at dinner next to Edgar Wallace, I don't know what they will say.'

(In another version of the same anecdote he used Hugh Walpole!)

Over time he necessarily grew accustomed to being interviewed and, while he clearly never enjoyed the experience, took it in good part. His wartime experience, however, raised a quiet *caveat*:

Writers on daily and weekly papers always will go all out for the picturesque. When they interview you, they inevitably alter and embroider.

As a rule this does not matter much. If on your arrival in New York you are asked 'What do you think of our high buildings?' and you reply, 'I think your high buildings are wonderful', and it comes out as 'I think your high buildings are wonderful. I should like some of these income-tax guys to jump off the top of them', no harm is done. The sentiment pleases the general public, and even the officials of the Internal Revenue Department probably smile indulgently, as men who know that they are going to have the last laugh. But when a war is in progress, it is kinder to the interviewee not to indulge in imagination.

(Letter to William Townend, 18 April 1953)

Later in life with American television came the celebrity author interview about which Wodehouse was predictably sceptical, when it was applied to him . . .

I don't imagine the great public listens spellbound . . . and says, 'My God! So that's Wodehouse! How intelligent he looks! What a noble brow! I must certainly buy that last book of his!' Much more probably they reach out and twiddle the knob and get another station.

(Letter to William Townend, 15 May 1947)

If they wanted to interview me on radio, that would be different. I have an attractive voice, rich, mellow, with certain deep organ tones in it calculated to make quite a number of the cash customers dig up the $3.50. But it is fatal to let them see me . . . I wouldn't risk twopence on anyone who looks as I do on the television screen . . . Say 1905 or thereabouts, I really was an eyeful then. Trim, athletic figure, finely chiselled features and more hair on the top of my head than you could shake a stick at . . .

He was to retain his down-to-earth perspective on the proper place of the popular writer in the literary food chain:

Every author really wants to have letters printed in the papers. Unable to make the grade, he drops down a rung of the ladder and writes novels . . . The truth is that a novel, after all, is rather a commercial sort of affair. A letter to the papers is Art for Art's sake.

('To the Editor, Sir . . .' from *Louder and Funnier*)

It has been well said that an author who expects results from a first novel is in a position similar to that of a man who drops a rose petal down the Grand Canyon of Arizona and listens for the echo.

(*Cocktail Time*)

But Wodehouse did admit to suffering from one professional problem that was probably unique to him. He was frequently interrupted in full flow 'because of Pekes who keep insisting on being placed on one's knee'.

* * * *

When Wodehouse wasn't actually writing, walking or nursing Pekes, he was almost certainly reading the work of other writers and his taste was catholic.

Not surprisingly, he had an early addiction to W. S. Gilbert and once, as a young man, disgraced himself at a dinner party by laughing uproariously at a Gilbert anecdote – before his host had reached his well-honed punchline. 'I had a rather distinctive laugh in those days, something like the last bit of water going down the waste-pipe in a bath . . . And it was at this juncture that I caught my host's eye. I shall always remember the glare of pure hatred which I saw in it . . . His eyes, beneath their beetling brows, seared my very soul.'

Gilbert might have been more sympathetic, had he been aware of one vital fact:

> It never pays to be honest with examiners. I lost an English Literature prize at school because I compared W. S. Gilbert to his advantage with Shakespeare. (I still think I was right.)
>
> (Letter to a fan, Mr Sheerin, 10 January 1974)

Dickens with his gallery of grotesques was, of course, another favourite, as, for more jingoistic reasons, was Kipling:

> Doesn't Kipling's death give you a sort of stunned feeling? He seems to leave such a gap. I didn't feel the same about Doyle or Bennett or Galsworthy. I suppose it is because he is so associated with one's boyhood. It has made me feel older all of a sudden.
>
> (Letter to William Townend, 20 January 1936)

. . . and there was an enduring affection for W. W. Jacobs:

> When I started out as a writer 72 years ago, W. W. Jacobs represented to me perfection. Others might abide my question, but he was free, as the fellow said. Even in my early

twenties, when my critical faculties were nothing to write home about, I could see how good he was and how simply and unerringly he got his effects, and nothing has changed in my high opinion of him since.

(Letter to Sir Hugh Greene, Chairman of the Bodley
Head, enclosing a promotional paragraph for a new book)

He became close – for him – to Sir Arthur Conan Doyle and greatly admired the Sherlock Holmes stories. References to them crop up frequently in the fiction . . .

'Ah,' said Mike, as a thunder of large feet approached along the corridor, 'here if I mistake not, Watson, is our client now.'

(*Spring Fever*)

I could never get him [Doyle] to talk of Sherlock Holmes, and I think the legend that he disliked Sherlock must be true. It is with the feeling that he would not object that I have sometimes amused myself by throwing custard pies at the great man.

(Introduction to *The Sign of Four*)

In one respect at least Wodehouse became a Holmes *doppelgänger*. Who wrote – 'Tell me the whole story in your own words . . . omitting no detail, however slight'? and who wrote – 'I must understand every detail . . . Take time to consider. The smallest point may be the most essential'?

Wodehouse wrote the first and Doyle the second. It evidently pleased one master to echo another, because over a period of some forty years Wodehouse used this precise word form repeatedly – 'Begin at the beginning and omit no detail, for there is no saying how important some seemingly trivial fact may be.'

'As the fellow said – there's no police like Holmes.'

On one occasion Doyle was telling Wodehouse how on a visit to America he had seen an advertisement for the 'Conan Doyle School of Writing' – a totally unauthorised organisation. His method of relating the story was what struck Wodehouse most:

> Well, what most people in his place would have said would have been, 'Hullo! This looks fishy.' The way he put it . . . was: 'I said to myself, "Ha, there is villainy afoot."'

The connection with Doyle was to have a postscript. Writing to biographer Hesketh Pearson (12 November 1944) to thank him for his new book on Doyle, Wodehouse recalls how Doyle had once asked him to find out who was the author of an attack on *Sir Nigel* (1903) in *Punch*. 'I found it was E. V. Lucas, one of his best friends, so not wanting to stir up trouble, I thought that the best thing was to pretend to have forgotten all about it!'

Literary feuds have always been commonplace but

Wodehouse drew a clear line of demarcation between the writer and his or her work. During the war A. A. Milne (he of Christopher Robin fame) wrote a virulent letter about Wodehouse to the *Daily Telegraph,* yet in a letter to Townend (27 November 1945) Wodehouse could still write:

My personal animosity against a writer never affects my opinion of what he writes. Nobody could be more anxious than myself, for instance, that Alan Alexander Milne should trip over a loose bootlace and break his bloody neck, yet I re-read his early stuff at regular intervals and with all the old enjoyment.

* * * *

Any English mystery, however bad, is better than any American story, however good.
(Letter to Denis Mackail, 25 December 1950)

Do you know, I think the greatest gift one can have is enjoying trash. I can take the rottenest mystery out of the library and enjoy it. So I can always have something to read.
(Letter to William Townend)

He was an avid reader of thrillers — particulary of the work of Agatha Christie and Dorothy L. Sayers. And — despite his misinformed dinner partner — Edgar Wallace ('Nine hundred of every thousand of Edgar Wallace's are worth the seven-and-sixpence every time').

Of the mystery genre:

> If I were writing a mystery story, I would go boldly out for the big sensation. I would not have the crime committed by anybody in the book at all.
>
> ('Thrillers' from *Louder and Funnier*)

> I hold strong views on them, one of which is that the insertion into them of a love interest is a serious mistake . . .
>
> Nobody appreciates more than myself the presence of girls in their proper place — in the paddock at Ascot, fine; at Lord's during the luncheon interval of the Eton and Harrow march, capital: if I went to a night club and found no girls there, I should be the first to complain: but what I do say is that they have no business in Lascar Joe's Underground Den at Limehouse on a busy evening. Apart from anything else, Woman seems to me to lose her queenly dignity when she is being shoved into cupboards with a bag over her head.

True, [Sherlock Holmes] would sometimes permit them to call at Baker Street and
tell him about the odd behaviour of their
uncles or step-fathers . . . in a pinch he might
even allow them to marry Watson . . . but
once the story was under way they had to
retire into the background and stay there.
That was the spirit.

('Thrillers' from *Louder and Funnier*)

* * * *

I always bar . . . the sort of story where
Chapter Ten ends with the hero trapped in
the underground den and Chapter Eleven
starts with him being the life and soul of a gay
party at the Spanish Embassy.

(*Thank You, Jeeves*)

*

He looked like one of those millionaires who
are found stabbed with paper-knives in
libraries.

(*Big Money*)

* * *

In the prisoner-of-war camp he became more interested in Shakespeare:

> Shakespeare's stuff is different from mine, but that is not to say that it is inferior. There are passages in Shakespeare to which I would have been quite pleased to have put my name. That 'tomorrow and tomorrow and tomorrow' thing. Some spin on the ball there . . . The man . . . could crack them through the covers when he got his eye in. I would place him definitely in the Wodehouse class.

And the fellow apparently suffered the same slings and arrows as every other writer:

> A thing I can never understand is why all the critics seem to assume that his plays are a reflection of his personal moods. You know the sort of thing I mean . . . *Timon of Athens* is a pretty gloomy piece of work, which means that Shakespeare must have been having a rotten time when he wrote it. I can't see it. Do you find your private life affects your work? I don't.

> (Letter to William Townend, 24 February 1945)

It would be interesting to know to what extent the work of authors is influenced by their private affairs. If life is flowing smoothly, are the novels they write in that period of content coloured with optimism? And if things are running crosswise, do they work off the resultant gloom on their faithful public? If, for instance, Mr W. W. Jacobs had toothache, would he write like Hugh Walpole? If Maxim Gorky were invited to lunch by Trotsky to meet Lenin, would he sit down and dash off a trifle in the vein of Stephen Leacock?

(*Love Among the Chickens*, 1921)

Wodehouse could turn out the stuff and that was all that mattered. When a correspondent grew pedantic because Wodehouse had quoted 'the ravelled sleave of care' as 'sleeve' in *Bachelors Anonymous* (1973), he got short shrift. 'Shakespeare couldn't even spell his own name, so I don't think we need worry about "sleaves" and "sleeves".'

Wodehouse was never notably enthusiastic about new developments in literature. For example, he doesn't appear to have shown much interest in modern American writers, though he did meet Scott Fitzgerald . . .

He was off to New York with [Ernest] Truex, who is doing his play, *The Vegetable*. I believe those stories you hear about his drinking are exaggerated. He seems quite normal, and is a very nice chap indeed. You would like him. The only thing is, he goes into New York with a scrubby chin, looking perfectly foul. I suppose he gets a shave when he arrives there, but it doesn't show him at his best in Great Neck. I would like to see more of him.

(Letter to Leonora Wodehouse, 14 November 1923)

What curious stuff the modern American short story is. The reader has to do all the work. The writer just shoves down something that seems to have no meaning whatever, and it is up to you to puzzle out what is between the lines.

(Letter to William Townend, 1 November 1946)

. . . and as for the novel . . .

I find myself more and more out of tune with the modern novel. All that frank, outspoken stuff with those fearless four-letter words. It was a black day for literature, I often think, when the authorities started glazing the walls of public lavatories so that the surface would not take the mark of the pencil, for the result was that hundreds of your literatteurs, withheld from expressing themselves in the medium they would have preferred, began turning the stuff out in stiff-covered volumes at 12s. 6d.

* * * *

Being of a naturally cheerful disposition himself, he found the Russian writers distinctly heavy going:

> No wonder Freddie [Rooke] experienced the sort of abysmal soul-sadness which afflicts one of Tolstoy's Russian peasants when, after putting in a hard day's work strangling his father, beating his wife, and dropping the baby into the city reservoir, he turns to the cupboard only to find the vodka-bottle empty.
>
> (*Jill the Reckless*)

If there was one thing worse than pretentious literature in the Wodehouse world, it would have to be the pretentious literary luncheon:

> It seemed to take one into a new and dreadful world . . . with other authors, mostly fairies, twittering all over the place, screaming, 'Oh,

Lionel!' and photographs of you holding the
book, etc. Gosh! Dumas was the boy. When
he had finished a novel he kept on sitting and
started another. No snack luncheons for him.

Had either of them taken a moment, they might have shaken a
fraternal head – in their respective languages, of course – at the
spectacle of the Algonquin Round Table at which Wodehouse
made a solitary appearance in his Broadway heyday. After which
he complained to Guy Bolton – 'All those three hour lunches
. . . when did those slackers ever get any work done?'

Nor is it likely that Dumas (*père* or *fils*) would have had any
more patience than Wodehouse for some of the figures on what
he saw as the fringes of literature:

The literary agent was a grim, hard-bitten
person, to whom, when he called at their
offices to arrange terms, editors kept their
faces turned, so that they might at least retain
their back collar studs

('Honeysuckle Cottage' from *Meet Mr Mulliner*)

*

All a publisher has to do is write cheques at
intervals, while a lot of deserving and
industrious chappies rally round and do the
real work.

('Leave It to Jeeves' from *My Man Jeeves*)

*

'You told them you were expecting to sell a hundred thousand copies?'

'We always tell them we're expecting to sell a hundred thousand copies,' said Russell Clutterbuck, letting him in on one of the secrets of the publishing trade.

(*French Leave*)

But one detects that — in his heart of hearts and although he dabbled in it himself from time to time — Wodehouse's deepest literary distrust was reserved for poetry and for *vers libre* in particular. 'He looked like a man who would write *vers libre*, as indeed he did' (*The Girl on the Boat*).

In 'The Fiery Wooing of Mordred' from *Young Men in Spats* he refers to 'the unpleasant, acrid smell of burned poetry'.

It was a poetic drama, and the audience, though loath to do anybody an injustice, was beginning to suspect that it was written in blank verse.

(*Jill the Reckless*)

*

'Is it *vers libre*?'
'Sir?'

'Doesn't it rhyme?'

'No, sir. I understood you to say that rhymes were an outmoded convention.'

'Did I really say that?'

'You did, indeed, sir. And a great convenience I found it. It seems to make poetry quite easy!'

(*The Small Bachelor*)

*

I don't want to wrong anybody, so I won't go so far as to say that she actually wrote poetry, but her conversation, to my mind, was of a nature calculated to excite the liveliest suspicions. Well, I mean to say, when a girl suddenly asks you out of a blue sky if you don't sometimes feel that the stars are God's daisy-chain, you begin to think a bit.

(*Right Ho, Jeeves*)

*

She could never forget that the man she loved was a man with a past . . . Deep down in her soul there was always the corroding fear lest at any moment a particularly fine sunset or the sight of a rose in bud might undo all the work she had done, sending Rodney hot-foot once more to his Thesaurus and rhyming dictionary. It was for this reason that she always hurried him indoors when the sun began to go down and refused to have rose trees in her garden.

('Rodney Has a Relapse' from *Nothing Serious*)

The poetry virus always seeks out the weak spot . . .

*

I may as well tell you, here and now, that if you are going about the place thinking things pretty, you will never make a modern poet. Be poignant, man, be poignant!

(*The Small Bachelor*)

*

Poets, as a class, are business men. Shakespeare describes the poet's eye as rolling in a fine frenzy from heaven to earth, from earth to heaven, and giving to airy nothing a local habitation and a name, but in practice you will find that one corner of that eye is generally glued on the royalty returns.

(*Uncle Fred in the Springtime*)

*

CHAPTER EIGHT

'Bring On the Girls . . .'

Broadway, the Great White Way, the longest, straightest, brightest, wickedest street in the world.

(*Psmith, Journalist*)

*

Musical comedy is the Irish stew of the drama. Anything may be put into it, with the certainty that it will improve the general effect.

('Bill the Bloodhound' from *The Man with Two Left Feet*)

*

Writing musical comedies is like eating salted almonds – you can always manage one more.

'If one is expecting to be treated fairly,' said the Duchess with a prolonged yawn, 'one should not go into the show-business.'

(*Jill the Reckless*)

*

I have always had just the sort of mentality which the music-hall satisfied. It took strong men to drag me to see Tree in *Julius Caesar*, but if Harry Tate's *Motoring* was on in Islington I was there in two jumps. Sentimentalising about the halls is the one sure sign of senile decay, and I do it all the time.

Even at the tender age of twelve, the music hall appealed to the artist in me . . . it was my earliest ambition to become a comedian on the halls . . . It was because a music-hall comedian required vim, pep, *espièglerie*, a good singing voice, and a sort of indefinable *je-ne-sais-quoi* — none of which qualities I appeared to possess — that I abandoned my ambitions and became a writer.

('Looking Back at the Halls' from *Louder and Funnier*)

* * * *

Wodehouse's theatrical career began in December 1904, when he was asked to write a lyric for a musical comedy called *Sergeant Brue*. It was a song on what was to become for him a recurring theme – the comical crook – and it was called 'Put Me in My Little Cell'.

On the strength of its success – ('Encored both times,' he confided to his diary. 'Audience laughed several times during each verse. This is fame.') – he was asked to work on another show. 'Regular job at £2 a week, starting with the run of *The Beauty of Bath* (1906) to do topical Gilbertian verses.' Since he was doing precisely this on a daily basis for the 'By the Way' column on *The Globe*, this was a painless introduction to the cut-throat world of lyric writing.

Working with him on the show was the young American composer Jerome Kern, with whom Wodehouse was to collaborate frequently a decade later. Their first number ('Oh, Mr Chamberlain') was sung by the leading actor-manager Seymour Hicks, and, although Wodehouse recalled it as being 'a pretty poor effort all round, but Jerry's melody was so terrific that the number used to get six or seven encores every night and I spent most of the next year writing encore verses'.

I would write encore verses for the old-fashioned type of topical song . . . with the sickening feeling at the back of my mind that by the time they were presented to the public they would be out of date and possess no meaning.

He was to dabble intermittently in other West End productions until he went to America in 1914 for what became an extended stay, when he was stranded there on the outbreak of war.

* * * *

In 1915 he was working for *Vanity Fair,* 'a swanky magazine devoted to Society and the Arts'. Wodehouse used to write anything up to five pages each month under a variety of pen names – Pelham Grenville, J. Plum, C. P. West ('which, incidentally, is about as good a pen name as anyone ever thought of') and P. Brooke-Haven among them. Since the magazine didn't take fiction, he had to make do with comic articles.

One of his many roles was Dramatic Critic and it was in that capacity that he visited the Princess Theatre on the evening of 23 December 1915 to review the opening night of *Very Good Eddie.*

The Princess was a small theatre by Broadway standards (it held only 299 people) but it was making a big experiment. In the face of the expectedly lavish musical extravaganzas – usually either British imports or adaptations of Middle European operettas – it was attempting 'chamber musicals' with small casts, orchestras and budgets and using contemporary themes. Without seeking to do so as deliberate policy, the principals were effectively inventing the modern American musical. One of the principals of this particular show was already known to Wodehouse – Jerome Kern.

From the back of the stalls Kern and his collaborator, Guy Bolton, anxiously watched the *Vanity Fair* critic to judge his reaction to their offering. He seemed to be favourably impressed, although in his diary he would write that he had 'enjoyed it in spite of lamentable lyrics'.

* * * *

It isn't easy for a man to register a great deal of emotion in a dark theatre when he's only got a bald head to do it with, but Mr Pottinger was making a darned good try.

('Back to the Garage' from *Strand Magazine*, July 1929)

* * * *

Kern and Bolton totally agreed about the *Very Good Eddie* lyrics and, when Kern introduced Wodehouse to Bolton a little later, it was suggested that they work as a trio in future. This they did intermittently for the next decade, as well as working with other writers and composers as the occasion arose. And arise it often did for those in demand. Wodehouse could claim to have been involved in more than thirty musical comedies between 1915 and 1928 alone. Kern had six shows running in one year (1917).

This 'trio of musical fame, Bolton and Wodehouse and Kern' (George S. Kaufman) began to craft the 'integrated musical' in which songs sprang naturally out of plot and character. Hitherto, it had been the habit to stop the plot arbitrarily and 'interpolate' a totally unconnected number in the hope that it might become an individual hit. Kern himself had done his share of interpolation and was heartily sick of the practice . . .

* * * *

Here, a composer who had not got an interpolated number in the show was explaining to another composer who had not got an interpolated number in the show the exact source from which a third composer who had got an interpolated number in the show had stolen the number which he had got interpolated. There, two musical comedy artists who were temporarily resting were agreeing that the *prima donna* was a dear thing but that, contrary as it was to their life-long policy to knock anybody, they must say that she was beginning to show the passage of years a trifle and ought to be warned by some friend that her career as an *ingénue* was a thing of the past.

(*Jill the Reckless*, 1921)

* * * *

One of the trio's first assignments was *Miss Springtime* (1916) for the diminutive but fiery Broadway producer Abraham Lincoln Erlanger, who might just as well have added 'Napoleon' to his roster of Christian names. He was, according to Wodehouse, a man 'who eats broken bottles and conducts human sacrifices at the time of the full moon'. He was also given to keeping a loaded revolver in his desk — 'no doubt in case he ever met the Duke of Wellington . . . Why shouldn't a fellow shoot a chap from time to time if the situation seemed to call for it? What's the sense of having a loaded revolver if you never use it?'

In the subsequent *Have a Heart* (1917) Wodehouse was to lampoon him – but not in an Erlanger show!

> *Napoleon was a homely gink,*
> *He hadn't time to doll up,*
> *But though he looked like thirty cents,*
> *He packed an awful wallop.*
> *And all the kings of Europe,*
> *When they came to know his habits,*
> *Pulled up their socks and ran for blocks,*
> *He got them scared like rabbits.*

In *Jill the Reckless* (1921) Erlanger appears as 'Isaac Goble' of Goble & Cohn . . .

He had been brought up in the lower-browed school of musical comedy, where you shelved the plot after the opening number and filled the rest of the evening by bringing on the girls in a variety of exotic costumes, with some good vaudeville specialists to get the laughs. Mr Goble's idea of a musical piece was something embracing trained seals, acrobats, and two or three teams of skilled buck-and-wing dancers, with nothing on the stage, from a tree to a lamp-shade, which could not suddenly turn into a chorus-girl. The austere legitimateness of *The Rose of America* gave him a pain in the neck. He loathed plot, and *The Rose of America* was all plot.

Why, then, had the earthy Mr Goble consented to associate himself with the production of this intellectual play? Because he was subject, like all other New York managers, to intermittent spasms of the idea that the time is ripe for a revival of comic opera. Sometimes, lunching in his favourite corner of the Cosmopolis grill-room, he would lean across the table and beg some other manager to take it from him that the time was ripe for a revival of comic opera — or more cautiously, that pretty soon the time was going to be ripe for a revival of comic opera. And the other manager would nod his head and thoughtfully stroke his three chins and admit that, sure as God made little apples, the time was darned soon going to be ripe for a revival of comic opera. And then they would stuff themselves with rich food and light big cigars and brood meditatively.

(*Jill the Reckless*)

'I've seen worse shows than this turned into hits. All it wants is a new book and lyrics and a different score.'

(*Jill the Reckless*)

* * * *

One of the more daunting tasks the *Vanity Fair* critic faced was reviewing his own Broadway debut . . .

I feel a slight diffidence about growing enthusiastic about *Miss Springtime,* for the fact is that, having contributed a few little lyrical bijoux to the above (just a few trifles, you know, dashed off in the intervals of more serious work), I am drawing a royalty from it which has already caused the wolf to move up a few parasangs from the Wodehouse doorstep. Far be it from me to boast — from sordid and commercial motives — a theatrical entertainment whose success means the increase of my meat-meals per week from one to two, but candor compels me to say that *Miss Springtime* is a corker. It is the best musical play in years.

For the next twenty years Wodehouse was actively involved in musical theatre on both sides of the Atlantic — all this at a time when he was also producing the substantial body of fiction for which he is best known. Not surprisingly, it got into his creative blood . . .

My heart was never really in [straight plays]. Musical comedy was my dish, the musical-comedy my spiritual home. I would rather have written *Oklahoma!* than *Hamlet*. (Actually, as the records show, I wrote neither, but you get the idea.)

*

Musical comedy is not dashed off. It grows — slowly and painfully, and each step in its growth either bleaches another tuft of the author's hair or removes it from the parent skull altogether.

*

Writing musical comedy is like eating cherries: you can always manage just one more. No matter how many commissions you may have on hand, and no matter how definitely you may resolve that nothing will induce you to touch another, when the moment arrives, you always fall.

. . . we stage-lizards, we drama-snakes . . . whose only fault is that we wished to elevate the American drama by contributing a few chunks of musical comedy to it.

Every time I meet Guy Bolton, we vow that we will go on the musical comedy wagon, but our resolution never comes to anything. Somehow we find ourselves in Mr Dillingham's office and there is the box of cigars on the table and Mr Ziegfeld in his chair by the window and everything jolly and homelike and innocent and then Mr Dillingham says casually, 'Wouldn't it be fun if we were to get up some theatricals just for a lark?' and Mr Ziegfeld says, 'Yes, wouldn't it?' and Mr Dillingham says he knows a place round the corner which he could hire for an evening or two, and Mr Ziegfeld says there's nothing like getting something to do in your spare time, as it keeps you out of the saloons and bowling alleys; and you get the general impression that you're all going to dress up and act charades for the children some evening later on; and then a voice through the smoke coos, 'Sign here, boys!' and you wake up on Broadway and find that you're going to do the next show for the Century [Theatre].

(*Vanity Fair*, September 1917)

He was to continue to be concerned for it as a genre long after he had ceased to be an active player:

If you ever catch me in pensive mood, sitting with chin supported on the hand and the elbow on the knee, like Rodin's 'Thinker', you can be pretty sure I am saying to myself 'Whither the New York musical-comedy theatre?' or possibly, 'The New York musical-comedy theatre . . . whither?' It is a question that constantly exercises me.

*

It became a constant point of reference for eccentric behaviour:
'I've always maintained and I always will maintain that for pure lunacy nothing can

touch the musical comedy business. Alice in Wonderland is nothing to it.'

'Have you felt that, too? That's exactly how I feel. It's like a perpetual Mad Hatter's Tea Party.'

(Wally Mason and Jill in *Jill the Reckless*)

*

[Bingo Little] always reminds me of the hero of a musical comedy who takes the centre of the stage, gathering the boys round him in a circle, and tells them all about his love at the top of his voice.

('The Pride of the Woosters is Wounded' from *The Inimitable Jeeves*)

*

'I hate you, I hate you!' cried Madeline, a thing I didn't know anyone ever said except in the second act of a musical comedy.

(*Stiff Upper Lip, Jeeves*)

At the end of the revue *Miss 1917* (1917) there is the following exchange between the hero and the heroine:

JOE: I've followed you through two acts and an intermission. Where have you been?

POLLY: I've been in the movies.

JOE: I should think from what I've seen of this show, that you've been in vaudeville.

POLLY: You've really followed me through all that maze of dancers and speciality people? Oh, Joe!

Even in 1917 there were premonitions of what was to come that would change Broadway and the theatre in general:

> *Dear old stage-door,*
> *You're not the same somehow.*
> *All the idols we used to worship*
> *Are in the movies now.*
> *On Wednesday afternoons*
> *We've nowhere to go;*
> *For there's no stage-door*
> *At the moving picture show.*

* * * *

There were all the genre stereotypes to be stirred. The Chorus Girl, for example:

'I regard the entire personnel of the ensembles of our musical comedy theatres as — if you will forgive me being Victorian for a moment — painted hussies.'

'They've got to paint.'

'Well, they needn't huss.'

(*Heavy Weather*)

*

'I was in musical comedy. I used to sing in the chorus, till they found out where the noise was coming from.'

(*Luck of the Bodkins*)

*

'They seem to think just because a girl works in the chorus she must be a sort of animated champagne-vat, spending her life dancing on supper-tables with tight stockbrokers.'

(*Summer Lighting*)

. . . and should the champagne go flat . . .

Today she resembled a Ziegfeld Follies girl who had been left out in the rain and had swollen a little.

(*Company for Henry*)

[*196*]

I love writing lyrics. For years scarcely a day passed whose low descending sun did not see me at my desk trying to find some lyric for 'June' that would not be 'soon', 'moon' . . . or 'spoon'.

He would complain — but not too seriously — about the problems the would-be lyricist faced:

Whoever invented the English language must have been a prose-writer, not a versifier; for he made meagre provision for the poets. Indeed, the word 'you' is almost the only decent chance he has given them. You can do something with a word like 'you'. It rhymes with 'Sue', 'eyes of blue', 'woo', and all sorts of succulent things, easily fitted into the fabric of a lyric. And it has the enormous advantage that it can be repeated thrice at the end of a refrain when the composer has given you those three long notes, which is about all a composer ever thinks of. When a composer hands a lyricist a 'dummy' for a song, ending thus . . .

Tiddley-tum, tiddley-tum,

> *Pom-pom-pom, pom-pom-pom,*
> *Tum, tum, tum . . .*

. . .the lyricist just shoves down 'You, you, you' for the last line and then sets to work to fit the rest of the words to it. I have dwelled on this, for it is noteworthy as the only bright spot in a lyricist's life, the only real cinch the poor man has.

(*On the Writing of Lyrics*)

Like Ira Gershwin – whom he considered pre-eminent among his successors in the field – he much preferred to fit the words to the music:

W. S. Gilbert always said that a lyricist can't do decent stuff that way. But I don't agree with him. I think you get the best results by giving the composer his head and having the lyricist follow him. For instance, the refrain of one of the songs in *Oh, Boy!* began: 'If every day you bring her diamonds and pearls on a string' – I couldn't have thought of that if I had done the lyric first. Why, dash it, it doesn't scan. But Jerry's melody started off with a lot of little twiddly notes, the first thing emphasised being the 'di' of 'diamonds' and I just tagged along after him.

Another thing . . . When you have the melody, you can see which are the musical high spots in it and can fit the high spots of the lyric to them. Anyway, that's how I like working, and to hell with anyone who says I oughtn't to.

By all accounts Kern was not a comfortable collaborator – and in his career he worked with over seventy lyricists. Wodehouse apparently brought out most of the best of him and remembered him fondly – 'In the Princess days he was one of the most cheerful and amusing men I have ever met, and an angel to work with, which many composers aren't.'

* * * *

By the 1930s Gershwin, Hart, Porter, Berlin and other indigenous American lyricists had taken over the Broadway musical, each of them happy to recognise the debt they owed to Wodehouse for showing that the rhythms of everyday speech could express everything that was needed.

And even a metropolitan audience likes its lyrics as much as possible in the language of everyday. That is one of the thousand reasons why new Gilberts do not arise. Gilbert had the advantage of writing for a public which permitted him to use his full vocabulary, and even drop into foreign languages, even Latin and a little Greek when he felt like it.

(*On the Writing of Lyrics*)

His last major show was to have been *Anything Goes* (1935). In the end it was reassigned to others – not least Cole Porter. When he heard of Porter's involvement, Wodehouse remarked – 'What pests these lyric-writing composers are. Taking the bread out of a man's mouth.' However, by the terms of the original contract Wodehouse and Bolton still received writing credits and were paid. Wodehouse wrote to Townend:

There are two lines of mine left in it, and so far I am receiving £50 a week each for them. That's about £3. 10s. a word, which is pretty good payment, though less, of course, than my stuff is worth.

To the end of their joint lives Wodehouse and Bolton were always hatching plans to write more shows together or revive old ones – a habit Bolton continued even after his friend's death. As early as 1937 Wodehouse is reminding him of 'what we have always said – that the way to get a hit is to take a couple of old hits and combine them'. Fifteen years later he can look back in nostalgia:

It is now just 40 years since we started
working on Broadway, during which time we
wrote twenty-three shows together and met
every freak that ever squeaked and gibbered
along the Great White Way. . . . I have
encountered . . . enough unforgettable
characters to fix up the *Reader's Digest* for
years and years.

He remained unduly modest about his own part in the
collaboration – 'I cannot recall one of them to which I
contributed anything of importance – except perhaps a few
lyrics.'

But the postwar Broadway Wodehouse encountered when
he returned for good worked in new, mysterious and mostly
unappealing ways:

I can't get used to the new Broadway [he
wrote to Bolton]. Apparently, you have to
write your show and get it composed and
then give a series of auditions to backers,
instead of having the management line up a
couple of stars and then get a show written
for them. It's so damn difficult to write a
show without knowing who you are writing
it for. It's like trying to write lyrics without a
book.

He was inclined to blame the politicians and the tax system:

> Old Pop Truman has properly put the kibosh on the angel industry. You would never believe the way these angels [backers] are covering up. I don't believe you could raise a cent for a show by God, adapted by Christ and the Holy Ghost.

To Gershwin he wrote on his Christmas card – 'Ira, we are well out of it.'

But then, in his heart of hearts, he was never to be truly 'out of it' and he was never so happy as when he could transfer his own trials and tribulations to one of his unfortunate characters. After all, if a writer can't act like some Great Producer-in-the-Sky on occasions . . .

> In order to make a song a smash hit it is not enough for the singer to be on top of his form. The accompanist, also, must do his bit. And the primary thing a singer expects from his accompanist is that he shall play the accompaniment of the song he is singing.

('The Masked Troubadour' from *Lord Emsworth and Others*)

He got through the song somehow and
limped off amidst roars of silence from the
audience.

('Extricating Young Gussie' from The Man with Two Left
Feet)

Among the papers found by his hospital bed after his death were
his jottings for new lyrics for *Kissing Time*, a show that he had
written in 1918.

* * * *

I have never regretted my flirtations with the
drama. They cost me a lot of blood, sweat
and tears, not to mention making me lose so
much hair that nowadays I am often mistaken
in a dim light for a Hallowe'en pumpkin, but
one met such interesting people . . .

Even though he wrote (usually in translation or adaptation) or
collaborated on more 'straight' plays than even a recognised
contemporary playwright like Frederick Lonsdale, Wodehouse
never – as he said – felt it was his principal *métier*. Perhaps it was
his introduction to the form that seared his soul . . .

My first play was written in collaboration
with a boy named Henry Cullimore when I
was seven . . . Henry said we would have to
have a plot. 'What's a plot?' I asked. He

didn't know. He had read or heard somewhere that a plot was a good thing to have,
but as to what it was he confessed himself
fogged. This naturally made us both feel a
little dubious as to the outcome of our enter-
prise, but we agreed that there was nothing
to do but carry on and hope that everything
would turn out all right. (Chekhov used to do
this.)

He got as far as —

ACT ONE

HENRY: What's for breakfast? Ham and
oatmeal? Very nice.

. . . but there he stopped. He had shot his bolt.
How he was planning to go on if
inspiration had not blown a fuse, I never
discovered. I should imagine that the oatmeal
would have proved to be poisoned — ('One of
the barbiturate group, Inspector, unless I am
greatly mistaken') — or a dead body would
have dropped out of the closet where they
kept the sugar. The thing was never produced. A pity, for I think it would have been
a great audience show.

Commercial reality sank in later:

> A successful play gives you money and a
> name automatically. What the ordinary
> writer makes in a year the successful
> dramatist receives, without labour, in a
> fortnight.
>
> (*Not George Washington*)

Nonetheless, there was a Wodehouse *caveat*:

> Brooding, as I do almost incessantly over the
> boneheadedness of the human race and the
> miseries resulting therefrom, I have come to
> the conclusion that much trouble might be
> averted if the Legislature had the sense to
> pass a law forbidding the dishing up of
> printed fiction in play form . . . I would make
> a few exceptions, of course, I would permit,
> for instance, such dramatisations as that of
> *Piccadilly Jim* —not only because it is impos-
> sible for such a story to have too wide a
> vogue, but principally because the author, a
> thoroughly worthy fellow, happens to be
> furnishing a new apartment at a moment

when there is an insistent demand on the part
of his family for a new car.

(*Vanity Fair*, November 1917)

There will, of course, be a few local difficulties to surmount in
rehearsal:

Any line that is cut out of any actor's part is
the only good line he has.

(*Jill the Reckless*)

There were certain plays that loomed large in the Wodehouse
canon. There was something about the 'Scottish play':

I don't know if you ever came across a play of
Shakespeare's called *Macbeth*? If you did, you
may remember this bird Macbeth bumps off
another bird named Banquo and gives a big
dinner to celebrate, and picture his em-
barrassment when about the first of the gay
throng to turn up is Banquo's ghost, all merry
and bright, covered in blood. It gave him a
pretty nasty start, Shakespeare does not
attempt to conceal.

('The Shadow Passes' from *Nothing Serious*)

*

His nose . . . was twitching like a rabbit's, and in the eyes . . . there was dawning slowly a look of incredulous horror. It was as if he had been cast for the part of Macbeth and was starting to run through Banquo's ghost scene.

(*Uncle Fred in the Springtime*)

*

His manner had nothing in it of the jolly innkeeper of the old-fashioned comic opera. He looked more like Macbeth seeing a couple of Banquos.

(*Frozen Assets*)

*

She came leaping towards me, like Lady Macbeth coming to get first-hand news from the guest room.

(*Joy in the Morning*)

*

The butler was looking nervous, like Macbeth interviewing Lady Macbeth after one of her visits to the 'spare room'.

('Buried Treasure' from *Lord Emsworth and Others*)

*

But throughout his whole career he was never really at ease in the medium of the 'straight play':

> I wish you would take my script and pull it to pieces and supply a new layout. I know my limitations so well as regards stage work. I think my dialogue is good, but, left to myself, I am apt to fall down on the story. I have never had a success on stage when I have written the story, and I have never had a failure when the story had been supplied by someone else. *The Play's the Thing, The Cardboard Lover* and *Candlelight*, all of which I adapted following the original story closely, were all big hits. So, if you can suggest a new story-line, I could dialogue it.
>
> (*Letter of 22 April 1951 to Prof. Conkle (University of Texas), with whom Wodehouse was attempting to collaborate on a play about headhunters.*)

There was a distinct touch of incredulous horror in the air when Wodehouse came to contemplate the 'kitchen sink' drama of the late 1950s, although there is absolutely no evidence that he ever actually *saw* any of it . . .

They had all gone on to the opening
performance at the Flaming Youth Group
Centre of one of those *avant-garde* plays
which bring the scent of boiling cabbage
across the footlights and in which the little
man in the bowler hat turns out to be God.

(*Service with a Smile*)

* * * *

In the last years of his life Wodehouse became a television
addict. Nothing – not even his writing – was allowed to come
between him and his 'daytime soaps'. Presumably one popular
entertainer recognised another successful formula when he saw
it. But it was not always thus.

In 1952 he was writing to Townend:

What a loathsome invention it is. You hear
people say it's going to wipe out books,
theatre, radio and motion pictures, but I
wonder. I don't see how they can help
running out of material eventually. The stuff
they dish out is bad enough now, and will
presumably get worse. (Not that you can go
by what I predict. I was the man who told
Alexander Graham Bell not to expect too
much of that thing he had invented called the

telephone or some such name, as it could never be more than an amusing toy.)

And later:

I sometimes think, looking back to the time when I was a viewer, that I could have endured television with more fortitude if they had not laughed so much all the time . . . The gruesome thing is that this is not always the laughter of a real studio audience. Frequently, it is tinned or bottled. They preserve it on sound tracks, often dating back for years, so that what you are getting is the mummified mirth of people who, in many cases, died way back in about 1946 . . . It used to be obligatory to laugh whenever anyone on the television mentioned Brooklyn . . . and now there has been a change of policy, and today you have to laugh at Texas.

You may have formed the impression that I dislike television. I would not go as far as to say that. Apart from thinking it the foulest, ghastliest, loathsomest nightmare ever inflicted by science on a suffering human race, it can carry on, provided – I say provided – I have not to excite the derision of the mob by appearing on the screen myself . . .

Were he with us to look back down the corridor of the years, he might find it mildly amusing to contemplate that several generations have discovered his printed prose, having first enjoyed seeing it adapted – for television.

CHAPTER NINE

Clubs and Codes . . .

'Sir Jasper Finch-Farrowmere?' said Wilfred.
'ffinch-ffarrowmere,' corrected the visitor, his
sensitive ear detecting the capital letters.

('A Slice of Life' from *Meet Mr Mulliner*)

*

Reluctant though one may be to admit it, the entire
British aristocracy is seamed and honeycombed
with immorality. If you took a pin and jabbed it
down anywhere in the pages of *Debrett's Peerage*,
you would find it piercing the name of someone
who was going about the place with a conscience
as tender as a sunburned neck.

('The Smile That Wins' from *Mulliner Nights*)

'Do you know what you are, my lad? You're an obstinate relic of an exploded feudal system.'

'Very good, sir.'

('Comrade Bingo' from *The Inimitable Jeeves*)

* * * *

Wodehouse's childhood visits with his assembly of 'aunts' had made him well aware of the social hierarchy of Victorian England. Well into the Edwardian era – in which he admitted himself to be happily stuck – it was perfectly normal for the well-to-do, quite apart from the aristocracy, to have 'somewhere in town' from which they could retreat to their 'country place'. It was a world with which Trollope or Wilde would have been perfectly familiar.

The characters he created were, of course, his own unique variations on established themes but the social rules by which they lived were – in the view of *their* creators – the bedrock on which society was built. And Wodehouse found them endlessly fascinating.

Turn a page and you turn up a peer of the realm:

I do realise that in the course of my literary career I have featured quite a number of these fauna, but as I often say – well, perhaps once a fortnight – why not? I see no objection to earls . . . Show me the Hon. who, by pluck and determination, has raised himself step by step from the depths till he has become entitled to keep a coronet on the hat-peg in the downstairs cupboard, and I will show you a man of whom any author might be proud to write.

With the occasional exception, they were destined for a comedy role in the Wodehouse 'musical comedy' world. For instance, it is hard to take a man seriously who has facial hair with a life of its own. . .

The Duke's moustache was rising and falling like seaweed on an ebb tide . . . foaming upwards as if a gale had struck it, broke like a wave on the stern and rockbound coast of the Dunstable nose.

(*Uncle Fred in the Springtime*)

*

If he had a moustache he would have looked like a baronet.

(*Spring Fever*)

*

He was fingering his moustache nervously,

like a foiled baronet in an old-time
melodrama.

(*Money in the Bank*)

*

A sort of writhing movement behind the
moustache showed that Sir Aylmer was
smiling.

(*Uncle Dynamite*)

*

Like all Baronets, he had table-thumping
blood in him.

(*Summer Moonshine*)

*

SLINGSBY: A man with noble ancestors
might possibly use a fish knife for the
ontray but he would never mop up his
gravy with his bread.

(*If I Were You* – play)

One could be fairly sure that he would have little aesthetic sense
and that his physical surroundings would reflect it:

Whatever is said in favour of the Victorians, it is pretty generally admitted that few of them were to be trusted within reach of a trowel and a pile of bricks.

(*Summer Moonshine*)

. . . on the other hand, they had a finely calibrated set of rules as to what one did and did not do:

It is a good rule in life never to apologise. The right sort of people do not want apologies, and the wrong sort take a mean advantage of them.

('The Man Upstairs' from *The Man Upstairs*)

*

He had had to ask him to stay, but he had neutralised the man's menace by cleverly having all his meals in the library and in between meals keeping out of his way. A host can always solve the problem of the unwanted guest if he has certain animal cunning and no social conscience.

(*A Pelican at Blandings*)

. . . and there are, of course, certain fixed points of reference that it does not do to question:

'I am not going to marry Lord Rowcester,' she said curtly. It seemed to Colonel Wyvern that his child must be suffering from some form of amnesia, and he sat himself down to jog her memory.

'Yes, you are,' he reminded her. 'It was in *The Times.*'

(*Ring for Jeeves*)

*

TONY: What does this so-called 'Social Life' amount to? Spending money you didn't earn for things you don't want, to impress people you don't like.

(*If I Were You* – play)

Perhaps the greatest impediment to the continued well-being of the aristocracy was the younger generation:

The British aristocracy is apt to look with a somewhat jaundiced eye on its younger sons.

('The Custody of the Pumpkin' from *Blandings Castle*)

*

Inherited wealth, of course, does not make a

young man nobler or more admirable; but the young man does not always know this.

(*A Gentleman of Leisure*)

This is the age of the specialist, and even as a boy, hardly capable of connected thought, he had become convinced that his speciality, the thing he could do really well, was to inherit money.

('Ways to Get a Gal' from *Dream World*, February 1957)

* * * *

But running a close second as a blot on the aristocratic landscape was the omnipresent Secretary. Of whom *primus inter pares* was undoubtedly the Efficient Baxter.

Rupert Baxter ('a swarthy-complexioned young man with a supercilious expression'), 'the Earl of Emsworth's indefatigable private secretary, was one of the men whose chief characteristic is a vague suspicion of their fellow human beings. He did not suspect them of this or that definite crime: he simply suspected them' (*Something Fresh*).

*

You may freeze a Baxter's body, but you cannot numb his active brain.

(*Summer Lightning*)

*

'That is Mr Baxter,' Lord Emsworth replied.
   'Looks a bit of a blister,' said George,
critically.

   (*Summer Lightning*)

But then, in Wodehouse the female of the secretary species is
scarcely less deadly than the male:

Her voice was as cold as her eye. Lavender
Briggs disapproved of Lord Emsworth, as she
did all of those who employed her . . . When
holding a secretarial post, she performed her
duties faithfully, but it irked her to be a wage
slave . . .

   (*Service with a Smile*)

*

Lord Emsworth was, and always had been,
allergic to secretaries.

   (*Galahad at Blandings*)

*

'She covers my desk with letters which she
says I must answer immediately. She keeps
producing them like a dashed dog bringing
his dashed bones into the dining-room.

Where she digs them out from I can't imagine.

(*Galahad at Blandings*)

*

There was always something about his secretary's voice, when it addressed him unexpectedly, that gave him a feeling that he was a small boy again and had been caught by the authorities stealing jam.

(*Service with a Smile*)

* * * *

The only sensible course of action for an embattled aristocrat was to take firm steps in the direction of one's club and seek commiseration from similarly situated colleagues:

The club was a richly but gloomily furnished building in Pall Mall, a place of soft carpets, shaded lights, and whispers. Grave, elderly men moved noiselessly to and fro, or sat in meditative silence in deep armchairs. Sometimes the visitor felt that he was in a cathedral, sometimes in a Turkish bath . . .

One of those birds in tight morning-coats and grey toppers whom you see toddling

along St. James's Street on fine afternoons,
puffing a bit as they make the grade.

('Ahead of Schedule' from *The Man Upstairs*)

*

There are clubs in London where talk is the
crackling of thorns under a pot and it is *de
rigeur* to throw lumps of sugar across the
room at personal friends, and other, more
sedate clubs where silence reigns and the
inmates curl up in armchairs, close their eyes

and leave the rest to Nature. Lord Uffenham's was one of the latter. In its smoking room . . . were some dozen living corpses, all breathing gently with their eyes closed and letting the world go by.

(*Something Fishy*)

*

The floor was crowded with all that was best and noblest . . . so that a half-brick, hurled at any given moment, must infallibly have spilt blue blood.

(*A Damsel in Distress*)

Not that rest and relaxation were the only activities in clubland. Food and drink had their proper place . . .

To attract attention in the dining-room of the Senior Conservative Club between the hours of one and two-thirty, you have to be a mutton-chop, not an earl.

(*Something Fresh*)

* * * *

The inner man looms large in the Wodehouse canon:

What with excellent browsing and sluicing
. . . and what-not the afternoon passed quite
happily.

*

[Galahad Threepwood] had gone blithely on,
ever rising on stepping-stones of dead
whiskies and sodas to higher things. He had
discovered the prime grand secret of eternal
youth – to keep the decanter circulating and
never to go to bed before four in the
morning.

(*Full Moon*)

*

He tottered blindly towards the bar like a camel making for an oasis after a hard day at the office.

('Life With Freddie' from *Plum Pie*)

*

For years everybody had been telling Eggy that it's hopeless to try and drink up all the alcoholic liquor in England, but he keeps on trying.

(*Laughing Gas*)

*

He died of cirrhosis of the liver. It costs money to die of cirrhosis of the liver.

('Success Story' from *Nothing Serious*)

*

I was so darned sorry for poor old Corky that I hadn't the heart to touch my breakfast. I told Jeeves to drink it himself.

('Leave it to Jeeves' from *My Man Jeeves*)

At times the stuff takes on a life of its own . . .

The stoppered bottle does not care whose is the hand that removes the cork – all it wants is the chance to fizz.

(*Money for Nothing*)

*

. . . one of those innocent-tasting American drinks which creep imperceptibly into your system so that, before you know what you're doing, you're starting out to reform the world, by force if necessary . . .

('The Artistic Career of Corky' from *Carry On, Jeeves*)

[He] addressed her in a voice like a good sound burgundy made audible.

(*Do Butlers Burgle Banks?*)

Depending on mood and circumstance, the liquor made audible might be 'old tawny port' – but as far as beer was concerned, he was inclined to agree with Kipling that:

A woman is only a woman, but a frothing pint is a drink.

(*Pigs Have Wings*)

. . . a sentiment that one may not continue to pursue with impunity . . .

The lunches of fifty-seven years had caused his chest to slip down to the mezzanine floor.

('Chester Forgets Himself' from *The Heart of a Goof*)

*

The Right Hon. was a tubby little chap who looked as if he had been poured into his clothes and had forgotten to say 'When!'

('Jeeves and the Impending Doom' from *Very Good, Jeeves*)

* * * *

Then when the delights of Pall Mall palled . . .

I knew quite a lot about what went on in English country houses with their earls and butlers and younger sons. In my childhood in Worcestershire and later in my Shropshire days I had met earls and butlers and younger sons in some profusion.

Hosts in English country houses are divided into two classes: those who, when helpless guests are in their power, show them the stables, and those who show them the model dairy. There is also a sub-division which shows them the begonias.

(*Uncle Dynamite*)

*

In all properly regulated country houses the hours between tea and dinner are set aside for letter-writing. The strength of the company retire to their rooms, heavy with muffins, and settle down to a leisurely disposal of their correspondence. Those who fall asleep try again next day.

(*Pigs Have Wings*)

*

[It was a country house dinner party.] No fewer than ten of Hampshire's more prominent stiffs had been summoned to the trough, and they stuck on like limpets long after any competent chucker-out would have bounced them. No doubt, if you have gone to the sweat of driving twenty miles to a house to dine, you don't feel like just snatching a chop and dashing off. You hang on for the musical evening and the drinks at ten-thirty.

(*The Mating Season*)

Whether the lady of the house was, in fact, a Lady, she always seemed to see herself as Lady Bountiful . . .

'I'd like to settle down in this sort of place and spend the rest of my life milking cows and taking bowlfuls of soup to the deserving villagers.'

(*A Damsel in Distress*)

*

'I've got to take a few pints of soup to the deserving poor,' said Myrtle. 'I'd better set about it. Amazing the way these bimbos absorb soup. Like sponges.'

('Anselm Gets His Chance' from *Eggs, Beans and Crumpets*)

*

'That girl, to my certain knowledge, plays the organ in the local church and may often be seen taking soup to the deserving villagers with many a gracious word.'

('Fate' from *Young Men in Spats*)

Charity — as practised by Wodehouse's aristocrats — was not an unmixed blessing, since the donors seemed to feel it conferred on them a mixed bag of seigneurial rights . . .

She looked like a vicar's daughter who plays

hockey and ticks off the villagers when they want to marry their deceased wives' sisters.

(*Laughing Gas*)

* * * *

The Country, it seemed, exerted a fatal fascination over the City Dweller, no matter in which city he dwelt . . .

It's funny about people who live in the city. They chuck out their chests, and talk about little old New York being good enough for them, and there's a street in heaven they call Broadway, and all the rest of it; but it seems to me that what they really live for is that three weeks in the summer when they get away into the country.

('At Geisenheimers' from *The Man with Two Left Feet*)

. . . even when that summer place is no further than Long Island and lives

'like the mosquitoes that infest it, entirely on its summer visitors'

(*Uneasy Money*).

Despite all the evidence to the contrary, the rural idyll persists in persisting . . .

It was one of those still evenings you get in the summer, when you can hear a snail clear its throat a mile away. The sun was sinking over the hills and the gnats were fooling about all over the place, and everything smelled rather topping – what with the falling dew and so on . . .

('Jeeves Takes Charge' from *Carry On, Jeeves*)

*

The spreading fields of wheat took on the appearance of velvet rubbed the wrong way as the light breeze played over them.

(*Spring Fever*)

*

Somewhere in the woods beyond the river a nightingale had begun to sing with all the full-throated zest of a bird conscious of having had a rave notice from the poet Keats . . .

(*Ring for Jeeves*)

Living there, however, was a somewhat different proposition:

You know how it is in these remote rural districts. Life tends at times to get a bit slow.

There's nothing much to do in the long winter evenings but listen to the radio and brood on what a tick your neighbour is. You find yourself remembering how Farmer Giles did you down over the sale of your pig, and Farmer Giles finds himself remembering that it was your son, Ernest, who bunged the half-brick at his horse on the second Sunday before Septuagesima.

('The Ordeal of Young Tuppy' from *Very Good, Jeeves*)

*

Except for an occasional lecture by the vicar on his holiday in the Holy Land, illustrated by lantern slides, there was not a great deal of night-life in Dovetail Hammer.

(*Cocktail Time*)

Except, of course, for the village pub(s) . . .

In most English country towns, if the public houses do not actually outnumber the inhabitants, they all do an excellent trade. It is only when they are two to one that hard times hit them and set the innkeepers blaming the Government.

(*Something Fresh*)

[*231*]

. . . and the occasional function at the Village Hall . . .

[It] was one of those mid-Victorian jobs in glazed red brick which always seem to bob up in these olde-worlde hamlets and do so much to encourage the drift to the towns. Its interior, like those of all the joints of its kind I've ever come across, was dingy and fuggy and smelled in about equal proportions of apples, chalk, damp plaster, Boy Scouts and the sturdy English peasantry.

(*The Mating Season*)

CHAPTER TEN

. . . and Clergy

I'm an agnostic. My attitude has always been, we'll have to wait and see.

Though he was not in any sense a churchgoer, the Church had an early and profound influence on the young Wodehouse. Four of his genuine uncles were vicars and, irrespective of which 'aunt' he was staying with, church attendance was compulsory . . .

Not only were we scooped in and shanghaied to church twice on Sunday, regardless of age or sex, but on the Monday morning at eight o'clock – eight, mark you – there were family prayers in the dining room.

('Fate' from *Young Men in Spats*)

There is ample evidence that the Bible (King James's authorised version) as well as Cranmer's Book of Common Prayer featured prominently at the Princes' and it is no coincidence that the poetic language of those two great works instinctively found early echoes in his own unique literary style . . .

* * * *

The cook burst into tears and said something about the Wrath of the Lord and the Cities of the Plain – she being a bit on the Biblical side.

('Ukridge and the Home from Home' from *Lord Emsworth and Others*)

* * * *

Wodehouse the writer was no respecter of persons – and constantly turned them until he saw their funny side – but he was particularly fascinated by the pecking order of parsons. The hierarchy of the Church never ceased to fascinate – most of his attention being devoted to the lowly Curate . . .

You know Mr Brotherhood, the curate. That nice young man with the pimples.

(*Uncle Dynamite*)

*

His trust . . . is like the unspotted faith of a young curate in his Bishop.

('The Amazing Hat Mystery' from *Young Men in Spats*)

Like so many vicars, he had a poor opinion of curates.

('Mulliner's Buck-U-Uppo' from *Meet Mr Mulliner*)

'They train curates to judge bonny babies. At the theological colleges. Start them off with ventriloquists' dummies, I shouldn't wonder.'

(*Uncle Dynamite*)

'She said he had got to steal the pig.'
   'And what did he say?'

'He told her to go to hell.'
'Strange advice from a curate.'
(*Service with a Smile*)

England was littered with the shrivelled remains of curates at whom the lady bishopess had looked through her lorgnette. He had seen them wilt like salted slugs at the episcopal breakfast table.

('Mulliner's Buck-U-Uppo' from *Meet Mr Mulliner*)

Keggs looked reproachful, 'like a bishop who has found his favourite curate smoking marihuana'.

(*Something Fishy*)

Anyone who has ever heard a curate at a village concert rendering 'Old Man River', particularly the 'He don't plant taters, he don't plant cotton' passage, with that odd effect of thunder rumbling in the distance, has little doubt that his spiritual needs are in safe hands.

Not that a vicar's lot was always a happy one . . .

The Bishop . . . was talking to the local Master of Hounds about the difficulty he had in keeping his vicars off the incense.

> ('Unpleasantness at Bludleigh Court' from *Mr Mulliner Speaking*)

*

[The Rev. Rupert Bingham] seemed subdued and gloomy, as if he had discovered schism among his flock.

> ('Company for Gertrude' from *Blandings Castle*)

*

The Rev. Henry looked as disturbed as if he had suddenly detected Pelagianism in a member of his Sunday-School class.

> ('Tom, Dick and Harry' in *Grand Magazine*, July 1905)

Interdenominational backsliding seems to have been a constant concern to Wodehouse clergy. In *Laughing Gas* it even affects the heroine who gives 'a sort of despairing gesture, like a vicar's daughter who has discovered Erastianism in the village'.

One can, of course, understand their concern. One slip and the dear old C of E could easily find itself in the same pew as Market Snodsbury, 'mostly chapel folk with a moral code that would have struck Torquemada as too rigid' (*Much Obliged, Jeeves*).

Worse – creeping atheism might set in . . .

She didn't like him being an atheist, and he wouldn't stop being an atheist, and finally he said something about Jonah and the Whale which was impossible for her to overlook. This morning she returned the ring, his letters and a china ornament with 'A Present from Blackpool' on it, which he bought her last summer while visiting relatives in the north.

(*The Mating Season*)

And *then* what would the Bishop have to say?

Anybody who has ever attended Old Boys' dinners knows that Bishops are tough stuff. They take their time, these prelates. They mouth their words and shape their periods. They roam with frightful deliberation from the grave to the gay, from the manly straightforward to the whimsically jocular. Not one of them but is good for at least twenty-five minutes.

(*Big Money*)

What's more their influence extends far beyond the spiritual into the realms of the commercial:

Just as all American publishers hope that if they are good and lead upright lives, their books will be banned in Boston, so all English publishers pray that theirs will be denounced from the pulpit by a bishop. Full statistics are not to hand, but it is estimated by competent judges that a good bishop, denouncing from the pulpit with the right organ note in his voice, can add between ten and fifteen thousand to the sales.

(*Cocktail Time*)

About his own religion he was deliberately ambiguous. Even though he told an interviewer late in life – 'I am a Spiritualist, like my friend Conan Doyle' and he had shown interest in Spiritualism from time to time over a period of years, it's much more likely that he was closer to the mark when he told another interviewer in the year before he died – 'I'm an agnostic. My attitude has always been, we'll have to wait and see.'

CHAPTER ELEVEN

Wodehouse in Wonderland

What a curious place this is . . . There's no doubt about it, this is the abode of the damned.

(Letter to Guy Bolton – 19 July 1930)

*

The best-laid plans of mice and men end up on the cutting room floor.

(*Pearls, Girls and Monty Bodkin*)

As a matter of fact, I don't think there is much to be written about this place. What it was like in the early days, I don't know, but nowadays the studio life is all perfectly normal, not a bit crazy . . . I don't believe I shall get a single story out of my stay here.

(Letter to William Townend, 18 August 1930)

* * * *

Wodehouse, in fact, played two engagements in Hollywood — which was remarkable in view of how the first one ended — and the time he spent there was probably the least productive of those pre-war years, at least in terms of what he was *supposed* to be doing. It was an experience he would share with many other 'real' writers as variously gifted as Scott Fitzgerald, William Faulkner and Dorothy Parker . . . the list was endless.

At the end of the 1920s Warner Brothers had given the movies their voice and now Hollywood — in a predictable panic — was reaching for those who presumably had the ability to put words into the actors' mouths. Money was no object.

On a brief trip in 1929 he had been a spectator of the surrealistic scene:

In every studio there are rows and rows of little hutches, each containing an author on a long contract at a weekly salary. You see their anxious little faces peering out through the bars. You hear them whining piteously to

be taken for a walk. And does the heart
bleed? You bet it bleeds. A visitor has to be
very callous not to be touched by a spectacle
such as this.

> ('Slaves of Hollywood', *Saturday Evening Post, 7 December
> 1929*)

But on 8 May 1930 Wodehouse – accompanied by his step-
daughter, Leonora – stepped off the train in Hollywood, ready
to transform the movie business.

It was an era when only a man of exceptional
ability and determination could keep from
getting signed up by a studio in some capacity
or another. I happened to be engaged as a
writer but I might quite as easily have been
scooped in as a technical adviser or a vocal
instructor . . . The heartiness and hospitality
reminded one of the Jolly Innkeeper (with
entrance number in Act One) of the old-style
comic opera.

You crossed the continent to find yourself cheek by jowl with all
the people you'd been cheek by jowl with back home:

New York till then had been full of authors
. . . You would see them frisking in perfect
masses in any editorial office you happened to

enter. Their sharp, excited yapping was one of the features of the first or second act intermission of every new play that was produced. And in places like Greenwich Village you had to watch your step very carefully to avoid treading on them . . . The demand for authors in those early talkie days was so great that it led to a revival of the old press-gang. Nobody was safe if he merely looked like an author.

****

You can't heave a brick in Hollywood
without beaning an English elocution
teacher. I am told there are English elocution
teachers making good money in Hollywood
who haven't even got roofs to their mouths.

(*Laughing Gas*)

*

A fellow I met in the canteen looked as if he
might be a writer of additional dialogue or
the man in charge of the wind machine.

(*Pearls, Girls and Monty Bodkin*)

* * * *

To begin with Wodehouse quite liked the place. After all, it was
as good a spot to work as any other and that was all that
mattered:

I have arranged with the studio to work at
home, so often I spend three or four days on
end without going out of the garden: I get up,
swim, breakfast, work till two, swim again,
have a lunch-tea, work till seven, swim for
the third time, then dinner, and the day is
over. It is wonderful. I have never had such a
frenzy of composition.

(Letter to William Townend, 26 June 1930)

[*244*]

The composition, however, was of his own stuff – not the studio's. ('I don't see much of the movie world. My studio – MGM – is five miles from where I live, and I only go there occasionally.')

Those occasional trips convinced him that he and his physical environment were not to be compatible:

I think California scenery is the most loathsome on earth – a cross between Coney Island and the Riviera – but by sticking in one's garden all the time and shutting one's eyes when one goes out, it is possible to get by.

As life goes on, though, don't you find that all you need is a wife, a few real friends, a regular supply of books, and a Peke? (Make that two Pekes and add a swimming pool.)

(Letter to William Townend, 28 October 1930)

It became abundantly clear to him at an early stage that the studio hadn't the faintest idea what do with him, now that they had him. It was also beginning to dawn on him that many of the studio executives not only didn't know what to do with *him* – they didn't know what they were doing. Period.

Imagine the effect of all this on a sensitive-minded author. Taught at his mother's knee to love the truth, he finds himself surrounded by people making fortunes by what can only be called chicanery . . . After a month or two in such an environment could you trust that author to count his golf shots correctly or to give his right circulation figures?

('The Hollywood Scandal' from *Louder and Funnier*)

* * * *

Mr Schnellenhamer of the Perfecto-Zizzbaum Motion Picture Corporation describes the play (*Scented Sinners*) he wants developed as a screenplay:

'Powerful drama of life as it is lived by the jazz-crazed, gin-crazed Younger Generation whose hollow laughter is but the mask for an aching heart,' said Mr Schnellenhamer. 'It ran for a week in New York and lost a hundred thousand dollars, so we bought it. It has the mucus of a good story. See what you can do with it.'

('The Castaways' from *Blandings Castle*)

*

When a studio executive charges you, look to the left but leap to the right. This baffles the simple creature.

(*Barmy in Wonderland*)

*

You can't go by what a man in my position promises. You don't really suppose, do you, that you can run a big studio successfully if you go about keeping your promise all the time.

(*Pearls, Girls and Monty Bodkin*)

* * * *

By now MGM, to Wodehouse's great surprise, had taken up the further six-month option on his contract and he was stuck, growing ever more frustrated that he was doing virtually nothing to earn his $2,000-a-week salary.

One small diversion was a visit to Hearst Castle at San Simeon — the folly built by newspaper magnate William Randolph Hearst in which he installed his mistress, Marion Davies, as hostess. Wodehouse had first met Marion in 1917, when — as an eighteen-year-old ex-Ziegfeld Girl — she had played an *ingénue* in *Oh, Boy!*.

An invitation from Hearst was greatly prized and the guests came in relays, a fact that was brought home to Wodehouse at mealtimes:

Meals are served in an enormous room, and are served at a long table, with Hearst sitting in the middle on one side and Marion Davies in the middle on the other. The longer you

are there, the further you get from the
middle. I sat on Marion's right the first night,
then found myself being edged further and
further away till I got to the extreme end,
when I thought it time to leave. Another day,
and I should have been feeding on the floor.

(Letter to William Townend, 25 February 1931)

So Wodehouse returned to Wonderland:

'You would like Hollywood, you know.
Everybody does. Girdled by the everlasting
hills, bathed in eternal sunshine. And if you
aren't getting divorced yourself, there's
always one of your friends who is, and that
gives you something to chat about in the long
evenings. And it isn't half such a crazy place
as they make out. I know two-three people in
Hollywood that are part sane.'

(*The Luck of the Bodkins*)

*

Everybody liked Bill Shannon, even in
Hollywood, where nobody likes anybody.

(*The Old Reliable*)

*

She had a sort of ethereal beauty; but then every girl you see in Hollywood has either ethereal beauty or roguish gaminerie or a dark, slumbrous face that hints at hidden passion.

('The Rise of Minna Nordstrom' from *Blandings Castle*)

* * * *

I got away from Hollywood at the end of the year because the gaoler's daughter smuggled me in a file in a meat pie, but I was there long enough to realise what a terribly demoralising place it is.

Well, it made a nice story but it didn't happen to be the whole truth.

As he was coming to the end of the extended contract, Wodehouse gave a routine interview to the *Los Angeles Times*. On 7 June 1931 their readers read the frankest comments about Hollywood any of its denizens had yet put into words:

They paid me $2,000 a week – $104,000 – and I cannot see what they engaged me for. They were extremely nice to me, but I feel as if I have cheated them. You see, I understood I was engaged to write stories for the screen . . . Yet apparently they had the greatest difficulty in finding anything for me to do. Twice during the year they brought completed scenarios of other people's stories to me and asked me to do some dialogue. Fifteen or sixteen people had tinkered with those stories. The dialogue was really quite adequate. All I did was touch it up here and there – very slight improvements.

Then they set me to work on a story called *Rosalie*

[Wodehouse had worked on the stage musical in 1928],

which was to have some musical numbers . . . When it was finished, they thanked me politely and remarked that as musicals didn't seem to be going so well they guessed they would not use it.

That about sums up what I was called upon to do for my $104,000. Isn't it amazing?

If it is only names they want, it seems such an expensive way to get them, doesn't it?

Naturally, my reputation is for light humour, jolly nonsense. I was led to believe there was a field for my work in pictures. But I was told my sort of stuff was 'too light'.

They seem to have such a passion for sex stuff. I wonder if they really know the tastes of their audiences.

The people who were most amazed by the interview were the studio money men back in New York. It gave them the excuse many of them had been looking for – in the aftermath of the Wall Street crash – to move in and clip the financial wings of their spendthrift West Coast colleagues. As he had said in an earlier context – Wodehouse Preferred began to look distinctly iffy in the eyes of Hollywood. When the Wodehouses left at the end of the year, he could hardly have expected to be back in a professional capacity.

Of course, my career as a movie-writer has been killed dead by that interview. I am a sort of Ogre to the studios now. I don't care personally, as I don't think I could ever do picture writing. It needs a definitely un-original mind. Apparently all pictures have to be cast in a mould.

(Letter to William Townend, 26 August 1931)

The movies are getting hard up and the spirit of economy is rife. I was lucky to get mine while the going was good. It is rather like having tolerated some awful bounder for his good dinners to go to his house and find the menu cut down to nothing and no drinks.

(Letter to Denis Mackail, 10 May 1931)

The only thing that excused the existence of the Talkies was a sort of bounderish open-handedness.

Destructive criticism is what kills an author. Cut his material too much, make him feel that he is not a Voice, give him the impression that his big scene is all wet, and you will soon see the sparkle die out of his eyes.

Once a combination of Santa Claus and Good-Time Charlie, Hollywood has become a Scrooge.

Do you realise that all that year I was away from London, when everybody supposed that I was doing a short stretch at Dartmoor, I was actually in Hollywood.

('The Hollywood Scandal' from *Louder and Funnier*)

* * * *

In the summer of 1936 Wodehouse received a surprising second offer from MGM. For years he had been led to understand that his name was synonymous with mud in Hollywood but, apparently, Time – which wounds all heels – had healed all wounds. The Wodehouses duly arrived on 10 October with a contract for $2,500 a week for six months and a further six-month option.

It was to be a replay of six years earlier. He was asked to work on a Jack Buchanan picture . . .

I altered all the characters to earls and butlers with such success that they called a conference and changed the entire plot . . .

The actual work is negligible . . . So far I've had eight collaborators. The system is that A gets the original idea, B comes to work with him on it, C makes the scenario, D does preliminary dialogue and then they send for me to insert class and what not, then E and F, scenario writers, alter the plot and off we go again.

You have to surround yourself with highly trained specialists – one to put in the lisps, another to get the adenoid effects, a third to arrange the catarrh.

('The Hollywood Scandal' from *Louder and Funnier*)

But what uncongenial work picture-writing is. It makes one feel as if one were working with one's hands tied. Somebody's got to do it, I suppose, but this is the last time they'll get me.

(Letter to William Townend, 24 June 1937)

It is only occasionally that one feels one is serving a term on Devil's Island.

(Letter to Denis Mackail)

Conscience was still gnawing at him:

The fact is, I'm not worth the money my agent insists on asking for me. After all my record here is eighteen months, with only small bits of pictures to show for it, I'm no good to these people. Lay off old Pop Wodehouse, is the advice I would give to any studio that wants to get on in the world. There is no surer road to success.

(Letter to William Townend, 6 May 1937)

What must have turned it into an out-of-body experience for him was the fact that the main project he was given to work on was *Rosalie*. The wretched woman seemed to haunt him. Then, to no one's surprise — least of all his — he found himself once more being moved into the wings. The story on which he had originally worked with Guy Bolton and the Gershwins was finally filmed – with music by Cole Porter!

To his relief, MGM chose not to pick up their option and

Wodehouse finished his second and last Hollywood stint in a rather happier frame of mind than might have been expected. RKO were about to make a film of his 1919 novel *A Damsel in Distress* and asked him to help out. Fred Astaire was to star with comedy team Burns & Allen, and he would be reunited with the Gershwins. As a tribute to their old friend, they had Astaire sing the title song in the grounds of Totleigh Castle, Upper Pelham Grenville, Wodehouse, England.

By August of 1937 his work was finished and he could write *finis* in a letter to Townend:

I don't like doing pictures. *A Damsel in Distress* was fun, because I was working with the best director here – George Stevens – and on my own story, but as a rule pictures are a bore.

On 28 October the Wodehouses sailed for Europe on the *Ile de France* . . .

2ND INTERMISSION

Style

One has to regard a man as a Master who can produce on average three uniquely brilliant and entirely original similes to every page.

Evelyn Waugh

Wodehouse's style cries out for one of his own original similes to describe its hybrid quality. It was like a well-worn suitcase into which a favourite Uncle had crammed the treasures of a lifetime . . . it was – but that way madness lies.

Sufficient that the man could take the ordinary image and the vernacular phrase and – as he would say – put a spin on the ball.

Waugh's favourite image was 'the acrid smell of burned poetry' (in 'The Fiery Wooing of Mordred', from *Young Men in Spats*). (Wodehouse returned Waugh's compliment – in typical Wodehouse fashion – by describing a character in *Frozen Assets* (1963) as resembling 'something unpleasant out of an early Evelyn Waugh novel'.)

Hilaire Belloc – best remembered for describing Wodehouse in the mid-1930s as 'the best living writer of English . . . the head of my profession' – chose 'quaking like a jelly in a high wind'. Biographer Frances Donaldson felt that nothing summed up Bertie better than 'the tall thin one with a face like a motor mascot' – though precisely what a motor mascot looked like she wasn't too sure. It is often the surprising rather than the particularly apposite Wodehouse image that has one 'staring incredulously, like one bitten by a rabbit' (*The Code of the Woosters*). You see how catching the whole thing is?

* * * *

She uttered a sound rather like an elephant taking its foot out of a mud hole in a Burmese teak forest.

(*Aunts Aren't Gentlemen*)

*

Her face now was pale and drawn, like that of a hockey centre-forward at a girls' school who, in addition to getting a fruity one on the shin, has just been penalised for 'sticks'.

(*Right Ho, Jeeves*)

*

He looked like a halibut which has just been asked by another halibut to lend it a couple of quid till next Wednesday.

('The Word in Season' from *A Few Quick Ones*)

*

IN HIS OWN WORDS

In *The Code of the Woosters* the arch-fiend, Roderick Spode has 'the sort of eye that can open an oyster at sixty paces', while in *Psmith in the City* a character 'scattered his aitches as a fountain its sprays in a high wind'.

*

> [The mass upon mass of bees] shoved and writhed and muttered and jostled, for all the world like a collection of home-seeking City men trying to secure standing room on the Underground at half-past five in the afternoon,
>
> (*Uneasy Money*)

* * * *

Not content with creating imagery, Wodehouse was given to inventing – or at least, modifying – language:

* * * *

> He spoke with a certain what-is-it in his voice, and I could see that, if not actually disgruntled, he was far from being gruntled . . .
>
> (*The Code of the Woosters*)

*

A sort of gulpy, gurgly, plobby, squishy, wofflesome sound, like a thousand eager men drinking soup in a foreign restaurant.

('Pig Hoo-o-o-o-ey' from *Blandings Castle*)

* * * *

It was the *sound* as much as the meaning of the word that seemed to appeal and the old Dulwich training came in handy when it came to ladling out the classical and foreign phrases. In the mouths of Bertie and his friends they often emerged a little mangled but usually managed to convey the *res*. Nor was Wodehouse averse to using them to enliven his correspondence. Reporting to William Townend on his meeting with Eleanor Roosevelt in October 1959, he says – 'We kidded back and forth with quite a bit of *élan* and *espièglerie*.' But always there is the sense that neither the speaker nor the hearer knows *quite* what the words mean.

When not hiding behind a smokescreen of pseudo-sophistication or erudition, the classic Wodehouse conversation is positively minimalist – the argot of the inarticulate:

> 'What ho!' I said.
> 'What ho!' said Motty.
> 'What ho! What ho!'
> 'What ho! What ho! What ho!'
> After that it seemed rather difficult to go on with the conversation.
>
> ('Jeeves and the Unbidden Guest' from *My Man Jeeves*)

> 'Yo-ho! Yo frightfully ho!'
>
> ('The Awful Gladness of the Mater' from *Mr Mulliner Speaking*)

* * * *

He had many stylistic parlour tricks that would be trotted out regularly. Some of them were almost – but not quite – the literary equivalent of the radio catchphrases so beloved of early audiences of the medium.

There was the mangled cliché:

'Break his neck.'

I nodded pacifically.

'I see. Break his neck. And if he asks why?'

'He knows why. Because he is a butterfly who toys with women's hearts and throws them away like soiled gloves.''

(*The Code of the Woosters*)

Wodehouse's abundant use of literary quotations might lead one to conclude that he was particularly well read. In fact, he was widely – but not particularly well – read. On closer inspection most of the references are the kind of tags with which a public-school boy of the period would be familiar.

The frequency with which he uses Shakespeare, for instance, is deceptive. One would deduce that 'sicklied o'er with the pale cast of thought' and 'quills upon the fretful porpentine' were required bedtime reading and for a Peke fancier he was remarkably fond of 'the cat i' the adage'. In fact, he only came really to study 'Shakespeare and those poet Johnnies' in prison camp. When he was packing, 'the very first thought that occurred to me was that here was my big chance to buckle down and read the Complete Works . . . a thing I had been meaning to do any time these last forty years, and about three years ago I had bought the Oxford edition for that purpose. But you know how it is. Just as you have got *Hamlet* and *Macbeth* under your belt, and are preparing to read the stuffing out of *Henry the Sixth*, parts one, two and three, something of Agatha Christie's catches your eye and you weaken.'

Nonetheless, that Oxford edition more than earned its keep:

'What's that thing of Shakespeare's about someone having an eye like Mother's?'
'An eye like Mars, sir, to threaten and command, is possibly the quotation for which you are groping, sir.'
(*Joy in the Morning*)

*

I felt that if the thing was to be smacked into, 'twere well 'twere smacked into quickly, as Shakespeare says.
(*Joy in the Morning*)

*

Bertie frequently believes that Jeeves himself came up with these insightful utterances:

Leaving not a wrack behind, as I remember Jeeves saying once.

The next moment I was dropping like the gentle dew upon the place beneath. Or is it rain? Jeeves would know.

And when Jeeves happens to invoke Dickens – 'It is a far, far better thing . . .' – Bertie's admiration knows no bounds. 'As I said before, there is nobody who puts these things more neatly than he does.'

And if the Bard was not sacrosanct, nor was anyone else with literary pretensions . . . There was Sir Walter Scott . . .

Oh, Woman in our hours of ease
Uncertain, coy, and hard to please.
When pain and anguish rack the brow,
A ministering angel, thou.

. . . and, of course, "the poet Burns", who – Jeeves was obliged to remind Bertie – "wrote in the North British dialect". . .

'Oh,' says the poet, 'what a tangled web we weave when first we practice to deceive', and it was precisely the same, Lord Emsworth realised, when first we practice to shoot airguns.

Byron's Assyrian, coming down 'like the wolf on the fold', is frequently invoked. Also Keats and his 'stout Cortez' with his 'eagle eyes whose men . . .

Look'd at each other with a wild surmise –
Silent, upon a peak in Darien.

. . . and, of course, the occasion when Bertie remarks to Jeeves that the morning seems very dark outside . . .

'There is a fog, sir. If you will recollect, we are now in autumn — season of mists and mellow fruitfulness.'

'Season of what?'

'Mists, sir, and mellow fruitfulness.'

'Oh? Yes. Yes, I see. Well, be that as it may, get me one of those bracers of yours, will you?'

'I have one in readiness, sir, in the ice-box.'

(*The Code of the Woosters*)

'You know your Shelley, Bertie.'

'Oh, am I?'

(*The Code of the Woosters*)

. . . and, Francis Bret Harte . . .

If, of all words of tongue or pen,
The saddest are, 'It might have been'

. . . Tennyson . . .

I don't know if you happen to be familiar with a poem called 'The Charge of the Light Brigade' by the bird Tennyson whom Jeeves had mentioned when speaking of the fellow

whose strength was as the strength of ten . . .
the thing goes, as you probably know,
   Tum tiddle umpty-pum
   Tum tiddle umpty-pum
   Tum tiddle umpty-pum
   and this brought you to the snapperoo or
pay-off which was 'someone had blundered'.
     (*Jeeves and the Feudal Spirit*)

Gally was hurt. He was feeling as the men
who brought the good news from Aix to
Ghent would have felt if the citizens of Ghent
had received them at the end of their journey
with a yawn and an 'Oh, yes?'
     (*Pigs Have Wings*)

(If they had, it wouldn't have been too surprising, since in
Browning's poem the 'good news' was taken from Ghent to Aix
– so to the citizens of Ghent it would have been 'old news'
indeed!)

. . . not to mention Kipling's 'toad beneath the harrow', which
knows 'Exactly where each tooth-point goes'.

* * *

There were the sheer inventions – usually in combined word
forms:

[267]

'Lady Constance spurned the grass with a *frenzied foot*' (*Heavy Weather*).' 'He waved a *concerned cigar*.' (*Jeeves and the Feudal Spirit*). 'I shot an *aghastish puff of smoke*.' (*Joy in the Morning*). A character in *Jeeves and the Feudal Spirit* was 'eating gooseberries in an *overwrought sort of way*' . . . while Bingo Little was 'standing on the steps, looking *bereaved to the gills*' (*Nothing Serious*). Muriel 'gnashed her teeth *in a quiet undertone*' ('The Voice from the Past' from *Mulliner Nights*) . . . while someone else '*groaned civilly*' (*A Few Quick Ones*).

. . . the unexpected adjectives . . . the transferred epithets . . .

'. . . like a bereaved tapeworm' (*Pigs Have Wings*) . . . 'like a smitten blancmange' (*Sam the Sudden*) . . . or, even worse, 'a pole-axed blancmange' (*The Inimitable Jeeves*) . . . 'one of the scaliest silences I've ever run up against' (*Carry On, Jeeves*)

. . . the surrealistic verb forms . . .

'You must *surge round him like glue*' (*Heavy Weather*). 'You must . . . *flock around her like a poultice*.' (*Right Ho, Jeeves*). 'I *trousered* the key' ('Jeeves Takes Charge' from *Carry On, Jeeves*).

Who, having once absorbed the image, can ever contemplate *leaving* a room again, when one can emulate Jeeves and . . . *shimmer* out? Or *walk* over to the Drones Club when to *toddle* or *ankle over* to the bally place is the –

'*Mot juste*, sir?'
'Precisely, Jeeves!'

Incidentally, at least one commentator has observed that when, in the first few pages of a novel, Wodehouse repeats the device of having Jeeves complete a quotation for Bertie or Bertie persistently uses abbreviations ('I could see at a g.' . . . 'the persp. was bedewing the forehead'), you are watching an old pro relying on the t. and t. (tried and tested) while he works himself into the swing of things.

(Ira Gershwin was paying lyrical tribute to this latter device when he wrote in the song 'S Wonderful':

> *Don't mind telling you*
> *In my humble fash*
> *That you thrill me through*
> *With a tender pash.*
> *When you said you care,*
> *'Magine my emosh;*
> *I swore, then and there,*
> *Permanent devosh.*

That was in 1927 but Wodehouse had been using it long since.)

* * * *

The lines on the printed page look effortless, as though they had leapt straight from brain to typewriter fully-formed. In reality, Wodehouse said – 'I'm always re-reading and re-writing what I've written. You put it down straight the first time. Then you fiddle with it, change it, change it again, and it gets better.'

CHAPTER TWELVE

Wodehouse's War

I'm not absolutely certain of my facts, but I rather fancy it's Shakespeare – or, if not, it's some equally brainy bird – who says that it's always just when a fellow is feeling particularly braced with things in general that Fate sneaks up behind him with the bit of lead piping. And what I'm driving at is that the man is perfectly right.

('Jeeves and the Unbidden Guest' from *Carry On, Jeeves*)

A great deal has been written about what happened to P. G. Wodehouse during World War II – too much in my view. Rereading it, I am struck by two things . . .

An unworldly man, who had come to live largely in the universe he had created inside his head, did a thoughtless thing, finally realised it and repented.

A lot of other people – many of them, it would seem, from motives of personal or professional jealousy – chose not to accept the obvious explanation, blew matters up out of all proportion and insisted on fanning the flames for the rest of Wodehouse's life and beyond.

In the process they might well have succeeded in overshadowing and undermining a unique literary reputation. Fortunately, the good sense of the bookbuying public saw things otherwise. As we entered the new millennium some hundred million books by P. G. Wodehouse in more than twenty languages had been sold around the world – which, in itself, says it all.

* * * *

Rather than extend the debate, I have simply selected from Wodehouse's own words spoken or written during that period. Clearly, any selective quotation is open to question but, then, I hope I have already made my own position known . . .

* * * *

Politics – at local, national or international level – were always transmuted into the narrative of Wodehouse fiction. On 4 September 1937 he is writing to William Townend from Hollywood:

What a hell of a mess the world has got into! I suspect plots all around me, don't you? I mean, this Japan business, for instance. My idea is that Italy and Germany said to Japan, 'Hey! you start trouble in the East and do something to make England mad. Then they will take their Mediterranean fleet over to Shanghai, and then we'll do a quick jump on their neck while they have no ships on this side.' I'll bet they're sick we haven't fallen for that.

By 23 April 1939 (to Townend from France) he must have been one of the few people who could conceivably have said:

> Do you know, a feeling is gradually stealing over me that the world has never been farther from war than it is at present . . . I think if Hitler really thought there was a chance of a war, he would have nervous prostration.'

> Incidentally, doesn't all this alliance-forming remind you of the form matches at school . . . I can't realise that all this is affecting millions of men. I think of Hitler and Mussolini as two halves, and Stalin as a useful wing forward. Anyway, no war in our lifetime is my feeling. I don't think wars start with months of preparation in the way of slanging matches . . .

> The ghastly thing is that it's all so frightfully funny. I mean, Hitler asking the little nations if they think they are in danger of being attacked. I wish one of them would come right out and say, 'Yes, we jolly well do!'

Came the 'Phoney War' – those first few months when everything seemed suspiciously like 'business as usual'. Except that some blighters were acting up. On 3 October, still writing from France:

> Didn't you think that was a fine speech of Churchill's on the wireless? Just what was needed, I thought. I can't help feeling that we're being a bit too gentlemanly. Someone ought to get up in Parliament and call Hitler a swine.

By 23 January of the following year:

> I agree with you about the weariness of war. I find the only thing to do is to get into a routine and live entirely by the day. I work in the morning, take the dogs out before tea, do a bit of mild work after tea, then read after dinner. It is wonderful how the days pass . . . My only fear is that Germany will be able to go on for years on their present rations. Apparently a German is able to live on stinging nettles and wood fibre indefinitely.

The Germans in his view, were in the same category as Hollywood producers – probably down to the accent.

Having completely underestimated the threat, the Wodehouses made no attempt to leave their French home in Le Touquet until the very last moment. In a scene straight from one of his novels, their car broke down and they were still there when the German forces occupied the area. On 21 July 1940 – aged fifty-eight – Wodehouse was arrested and interned, before being transported to a prisoner-of-war camp in a lunatic asylum in Tost, Upper Silesia. He stayed there until he was released, shortly before his sixtieth birthday – a mandatory release date – on 21 June 1941. He was kept in Germany for the next two years. After his release came the five broadcasts which were to cause the furore.

It was not until 11 May 1942 that he could reply to the many letters Townend had been sending to him in the camp. To Wodehouse it seems to have been Dulwich Revisited and he might easily have been writing home to his parents:

Camp was really great fun . . . I played cricket again after twenty-seven years, and played havoc with the opposition with slow leg-breaks . . . We used to play with a string ball (string wound round a nut) which our sailors manufactured.

He later referred to 'my beloved Tost, where life was one long round of cricket, lectures, entertainments and Red Cross parcels'.

None of which interfered with his writing:

I used to sit on my typewriter case with the machine balanced on a suitcase and work away with two German soldiers standing behind me with guns, breathing down the back of my neck. They seemed fascinated by this glimpse into the life literary.

By contrast he found the time in Berlin dull:

It's extraordinarily hard to describe my life there. I suppose I was in the middle of all sorts of interesting things, but they didn't touch me . . . I lived the life of a hermit, plugging away at my writing.
(30 December 1944)

In the autumn of that year the Wodehouses had been transferred to Paris for some reason and they were there when the city was finally liberated. It was only now that he became fully aware of the arguments that were raging around his head and the attacks on him in the British press, many of them based on imaginary interviews . . .

I wish, by the way, when people invent scenes with one, that they wouldn't give one such rotten dialogue. Can you imagine me saying some of the things he puts into my mouth? But I suppose there is nothing to be done about it now.

In Paris, with the war clearly winding to a close, he had time to contemplate the longer-term consequences of the broadcasts. Townend had written, suggesting that he felt the negative newspaper comment was starting to fall off. On 15 February 1945 Wodehouse replied:

It's fine if the papers are beginning to change their attitude. But I'm afraid there is a long way to go before things can come right, but I haven't a twinge of self-pity. I made an ass of myself, and must pay the penalty.

In May he was able to pick up his correspondence with Guy Bolton. His top news item was, predictably, his work:

I have been working steadily all through these troubled years, and now have four novels and ten short stories in my drawer.

. . . but he soon reverts to the broadcasts. Bolton had been very active in organising US opinion on behalf of Wodehouse's early release and it was gratitude for this action – one that had no UK parallel, by the way – that decided Wodehouse on making the broadcasts, ostensibly only to American audiences. In a letter of 1 September 1945:

It never occurred to me that there could be any harm in doing this, and I particularly

wanted to do something in acknowledge-
ment of all the letters I had had from
American readers, so I jumped at it . . . Isn't
it the damnedest thing how Fate lurks to sock
you with the stuffed eelskin . . .

To Ira Gershwin he added:

I thought it a good idea at the time, but have
since changed my mind. I suppose I was in an
unbalanced mental state after a year behind
barbed wire, but that was all I actually did —
give five short descriptions of life in camp,
purely designed as entertainment for the
boys in the U.S.A.

He speculated to Townend on his concerns about public
opinion:

You know how one's moods change from day
to day. I go for a walk and work up a spirit of
defiance and come home and write a
belligerent page or two indicating that I don't
give a damn whether the public takes a more
favourable view or not, because all my
friends have stuck to me and it's only friends
I care about. Then I sleep on it and wonder if

this is quite judicious! Also, comedy will keep creeping in and at the most solemn moments. I wrote this yesterday:

'The global howl that went up as the result of my indiscretion exceeded in volume and intensity anything I had experienced since the time in my boyhood when I broke the curate's umbrella and my aunts started writing letters to one another about it.'

. . . What do you think? Will the reaction be 'Ha, ha. I don't care what this chap has done. He makes me laugh' or 'Mr Wodehouse appears to imagine that his abominable action is a subject for flippancy.' You see. It might go either way, and I can't tell in advance . . .

And there – in Wodehouse's own words and between the lines – I believe you have what he would call the *res*. One could, I suppose, argue that this is a clever writer seeding his personal correspondence in the expectation of eventual publication but that is to attribute a deviousness he was never to demonstrate in any other context in an extraordinarily long life.

Personally, I am persuaded that Wodehouse's friend and wartime inquisitor, Malcolm Muggeridge, had it about right when he concluded:

It was an act of folly. But it was a product of his peculiar temperament. It wasn't that he was other-worldly, or un-worldly, as much as that he was a-worldly; a born neutral in relation to the conflicts, individual and collective, which afflict mankind.

By April 1947 the Wodehouses had been granted their American visas. Ethel couldn't contemplate the journey without first taking a side trip to London, naturally, on her own. ('She reported that things weren't as bad as she had been led to expect. But then she had a suite at The Ritz, and I imagine you don't see the real stark modern London life there.') On the 18th they joined the *S.S America* at Cherbourg. Except in his fertile imagination Wodehouse never made the return trip . . .

* * * *

Even though the official papers have now been released, the occasional intriguing footnote to the episode still appears. As late as 12 October 1966 Wodehouse sent to his son-in-law, Peter Cazalet, a copy of a letter he had received from an old Hollywood friend, Gene Markey.

Markey had apparently met Major Victor Cazalet at a social gathering in 1943 and Cazalet had taken him aside to say:

This is extremely confidential, but as you're a friend of Plum's, you'll be glad to hear that something is about to break, something very good for Plum, which will affect his status as a prisoner of war and be greatly to his advantage. I have just got hold of this information and I'm on my way to London to give it to the top boys.

Markey went on to add:

He couldn't tell me what it was, but said I'd be reading about it when the story was released. He had to take a plane at midnight, and I walked out to the car with him and said goodbye. He flew to Gibraltar, the plane crashed and he was killed. And the good news about you that he was taking to London never reached there.

CHAPTER THIRTEEN

*Uncle Plum in the Autumn**

My earnest hope is that the entire remainder of my existence will be one round of unruffled monotony.

(*Thank You, Jeeves*)

*

Like Jeeves, I know my place, and that place is down at the far end of the table among the scurvy knaves and scullions.

(*Over Seventy*)

*

In the course of a long life I have flitted about a bit. I have had homes in Mayfair, in Park Avenue, New York, in Beverly Hills, California, and other posh localities, but I have always been a suburbanite at heart, and it is when I get a plot calling for a suburban setting that I really roll up my sleeves and give of my best.

(Preface to *Sam the Sudden*)

*Should any Americans happen to read this, make that —
UNCLE PLUM IN THE FALL.

(*Positively the final footnote!*)

The world only knows him as he wishes to be known.

(David Jasen)

I look in my glass, dear reader, and what do I see? Nothing so frightfully hot, believe me. The face is slablike, the ears are large and fastened on at right-angles. Above the eyebrows comes a stagnant sea of bald forehead, stretching away into the distance with nothing to relieve it but a few wisps of lonely hair. The nose is blobby, the eyes dull, like those of a fish not in the best of health. A face, in short, taking it for all in all, which should be reserved for the gaze of my nearest and dearest who, through long habit, have got used to it and can see through to the pure white soul beneath. At any rate, a face not to be scattered about at random and come upon suddenly by nervous people and invalids.

I myself . . . am − strictly speaking − no Ronald Colman . . . But do not be too hasty. Wait a bit. See me first in my new autumn suit with the invisible blue stripe. Suspend judgment till my last lot of collars come from

the makers. Ah! you hesitate. Exactly. Mine
is a style of beauty that grows on you. It has
to have time to get its effect.

('On Ocean Liners' from *Louder and Funnier*)

* * * *

Even before the war he never thought would happen happened,
Wodehouse was getting restive to return to America.

In December 1939, now ensconced at Le Touquet – and
clearly oblivious to the threat just the other side of the Maginot
Line – he is writing to his old sparring partner, Guy Bolton:

I am longing to come over and get down to it.
We could turn out a terrific amount of work
collaborating. We might do a straight play as
well as musicals.

Six years later he is still stuck in France but finally the elusive
visas – like the 'letters of transit' in *Casablanca* – come through
and the final (thirty-year) chapter in Wodehouse's life begins:

Isn't it marvellous about the visa! Apart from
the fact that I am now able to come to
America, there is the other angle – that if the
US Govt., after reading the facts as supplied
by the British Govt., have come to the
conclusion that it was all right admitting me

to the USA, there couldn't be much in those
facts to kick at. In other words, the British
Govt. have practically given me a clearance.

(Letter to Guy Bolton, 13 July 1946)

On the eve of one world war he had made a decisive trip to the
US; in the aftermath of another he returned there for good.

Apart from Ethel, Bolton was to be the rock on which that
last third of his life would be built. 'You only need one friend,'
he once said. Bolton was that friend. In extreme old age Bolton
– who died in 1979 at ninety-five – was to say that it was only
Wodehouse's continued presence on the planet that kept him
going. They were friends and near neighbours on Long Island,
meeting virtually every day to work or walk – and often both.

As soon as he got back into the swing of New York life,
Wodehouse was full of plans for their renewed collaboration:

And now how are the chances of a musical by
us? I have abandoned all other forms of work
and am spending my whole time working on
lyrics and am pleased to report that the old
Muse is in the real 1916–1918 form . . . Of
course, the difficulty is that one is so
handicapped, working this way without a
story and characters . . .

A fear that haunts me, of course, is that I
may be thirty years behind the times and be
turning out stuff that would have been fine

for 1917 but no good for 1946. But I don't believe there is any reason to feel like this. The numbers I hear on the radio sound exactly like those of twenty and thirty years ago. My theory is that the business of keeping up to date is entirely the headache of the composer. If he is modern and the lyricist does his lyric to the music, the lyricist can't go wrong . . . Anyway, I'm working away like the dickens.

(Letter to Guy Bolton, 9 January 1946)

He was soon back in the old routine and relieved to be so:

I was thinking it over the other day and was surprised to find that I couldn't recall a single day in the last twenty years when I have been bored. I find that I get into a routine of work and walks and reading which makes the time fly. I never want to see anyone — except you, of course — and I never want to go anywhere or do anything.

(Letter to Bolton, 7 March 1946)

Although he did stumble across *one* new hobby of sorts . . .

I think my vicissitudes must have soured a once sunny nature, for nowadays I seem to spend my time looking about me for people to sue. A man here wrote a book about building a house and called it *Mr Blandings Builds His Castle*. I would have dismissed it just as a pretty compliment, but my lawyer said there was gold in them thar hills and wrote a stiff letter demanding compensation. His lawyers offered $100 and mine rejected that scornfully and finally worked them up to $1,500, which is pretty nice sugar. I am now suing the Kleenex people for using Jeeves in their advertisements and trying to think of somebody else to persecute.

(Letter to Thelma Cazalet-Keir, 18 December 1947)

In 1952 they bought a house in Remsenburg, New York State:

There are lots of nice drives you can take, but the catch is that if you want to go anywhere when you are living in Remsenburg, you have to do it by car, so the Wodehouse home is in ferment at the moment, everybody except Squeaky, the Pekinese, starting to drive.

Bunny used to be a very good driver, but

hasn't driven for a long time. Peggy, our maid, used to drive in Ireland when she was small and has started taking lessons. It must be 35 years since I drove and I doubt if I would have the nerve to do it today . . . When we were first married we had a little Chevrolet two-seater, and I think that's what we want now. I myself am going to buy a bicycle!

(Letter to Sheran Cazalet, 25 May 1952)

Once the Wodehouses were settled in, their natural propensity for Pekes evolved into providing a home for sundry other stray cats and dogs – all of whom (in his indulgent estimation) required the Wodehouse presence:

The whole point of buying this house was that we would have a place where we could turn the key and go away whenever we wanted to, and now I don't see how we are ever going to move even for a day.

(Letter to Denis Mackail, 8 July 1952)

It was ostensibly a complaint but the tone seems tinged with relief. To Bolton he wrote:

You and I were mugs not to go in for huntin' and fishin' in our youth or at least to have developed a fondness for bridge like S. Maugham. The only thing that we both did that was smart was to take up Pekes.

(Letter to Guy Bolton, 15 April 1950)

They continued to work – separately and together – with rather mixed results. Wodehouse continued to produce his comic novels at the rate of about one a year. He was finding the work took more out of him as the years went by but the critics on both sides of the Atlantic saw no diminution in the standard of the finished product. On the other hand, little of what the Wodehouse/Bolton collaboration produced came to anything – except the basis for the occasional gag:

Any time he has a good idea for a play, I am always ready to help him out. He knows that he can count on my support. It is not always convenient for me to stroll round the corner from my home to his and say, 'How are you getting on?' but I never fail him.

We are the closest of friends. If Guy saw me drowning, he would dive in to the rescue without a moment's hesitation, and if I saw Guy drowning, I would be the first to call for assistance.

(Introduction to Bolton's *Gracious Living, Limited*)

* * * *

Wodehouse badly wanted another Broadway success and
worried about his failure to achieve it like a Peke with a bone:

> I know just what is wrong with my stuff for
> the American stage. American audiences
> want plays about the relationship of men and
> women, while I write about some kind of
> venture like finding a diary or smuggling
> jewels and so on. It's all right in novel form,
> because I can nurse the thing along with a lot
> of in-between stuff, giving them the old
> personality, as it were, but for a stage play I
> doubt if you can get by with a story that
> doesn't deal primarily with sex relations. My
> type of story is apt to be thin on the stage. So
> why don't we try to get something sexy for a
> Jeeves play?
>
> (Letter to Guy Bolton, 5 February 1951)

Wodehouse went to considerable pains to cultivate the image of
a man who was largely unaware of what went on around him
and, by and large, it served him well. From the letters,
however, it is clear that his commercial sense was very much of
this world:

> My last book lost money and Doubleday [his

American publishers] . . . write to say that they will be obliged to reduce my advance. To which I have replied Like Hell you'll reduce my advance, adding that I consider them lousy publishers who never do a thing to push an author and am going elsewhere with my next. Curse and blast them! In the course of the years they have sold a million and a half of my books, and now this!

(Letter to Denis Mackail, 14 December 1952)

* * * *

In the early 1950s William Townend, his old Dulwich friend and lifelong correspondent, came up with the idea of publishing a selection of their letters. Wodehouse warmed to the idea as a way to create a form of autobiography without having to commit himself to something too formal.

As usual, though, he covered his tracks when he read the first draft:

The impression these letters have left me with is the rather humbling one that I am a bad case of arrested mental development. Mentally, I seem not to have progressed a step since I was eighteen. With world convulsions happening every hour on the hour, I appear to be still the rather backward

lad I was when we brewed our first cup of tea
in our study together, my only concern being
the outcome of a Rugby football match.

(Letter to William Townend, 18 April 1953)

He was – he would always claim – 'a not very complex man'.
Which, coming from a man of his achievements, is a more
complex thought than it at first appears.

It was – as David Jasen says – the way he wished to appear.
It was true enough, as far as it went, and it was a convenient
persona he sustained to the end.

He *was* a naturally self-contained man and increasing age and
his chosen geographical isolation made him more so:

Another very marked change I notice in the
senile Wodehouse is that I no longer have the
party spirit. As a young man I used to enjoy
parties, but now they have lost their zest . . .
Why people continue to invite me I don't
know . . . Cornered at one of these affairs by
some dazzling creature who looks brightly at
me, expecting a stream of good things from
my lips, I am apt to talk guardedly about the
weather, with the result that before long I am
left on one leg in a secluded corner of the
room in the grip of that disagreeable feeling
that nobody loves me.

He also perfected a *modus operandi* all his own when he decided it was time to leave a party. In *Carry On, Jeeves* Bertie says of Jeeves — 'He seemed to flicker and wasn't there any more.' In Wodehouse family circles this became known as the Wodehouse Glide.

This morning they are putting in the bar in a small room on the other side of the house. God knows why we want a bar . . . What is supposed to happen is that the County saunter in for a drink, and we mix it at the bar. The County little knows that if they come within a mile of us, we shall take to the hills.

* * * *

My wife tries to drag me to routs and revels from time to time, but I toss my curls at her and refuse to stir. I often think that the ideal life would be to have plenty of tobacco and be cut by the County.

(*Uncle Dynamite*)

His face wore the strained, haggard look it wears when he hears that guests are expected for the weekend.

Fortunately, the Gods were inclined to be kind . . .

> You will be grieved to hear that my monastic
> seclusion is being gradually broken into.
> Nella has made friends with a woman who
> lives next door to the Post Office and last
> Sunday we were all going to dinner at her
> house in spite of my protests. By great good
> luck the worst blizzard in eighteen years
> broke loose, so the date was scratched.
>
> (Letter to Edward Cazalet, 6 February 1966)

When there were guests at Remsenburg there would be the
occasional game of bridge in which Wodehouse would take
part. His grand-daughter recalls that he was 'a pretty moderate
player' but never particularly engaged in the pursuit. On one
occasion he was asked by his partner why in the previous hand
he had not played his ace earlier.

'Oh, I played it as soon as I found it.'

* * * *

He would often return in correspondence to his list of 'needs'.
In 1930 it was 'about two real friends, a regular supply of
books, and a Peke' – which, Hollywood being Hollywood, after
all, he amended to 'two Pekes and a swimming pool'. In 1932
he examined his soul, as he put it, and added 'a library
subscription and tobacco money, plus an extra bit for holidays'.

By the Remsenburg years he has reduced the 'two friends' to

one and in 1960 he is telling that one (Bolton) about his unvarying routine:

> Work in the morning, at twelve watch a television serial in which I am absorbed, lunch, take the dog to the post office, which covers two till three, brood on work till five, bath, cocktails, dinner, read and play two-handed bridge and the day is over. The same routine day after day, and somehow it never gets monotonous.
>
> (Letter to Guy Bolton, 6 June 1960)

Despite his earlier strictures, television managed to infiltrate and become an important part of his regimen:

> It is now three minutes to twelve, so I must go and watch *Love of Life*.
>
> (Letter to Guy Bolton, 6 June 1964)

> *Edge of Night*, which was rotten for a time but has now bucked up, a girl having been found in the doctor's bed stabbed with a carving knife (doc not yet arrested but going through a bad spell).
>
> (Letter to Edward Cazalet, 1 November 1970)

* * * *

Wodehouse was no longer a young man. He was sixty-five when he returned to America and as he approached seventy, health became a minor irritation, if not, as yet, a real problem. He began to suffer attacks of giddiness:

> The score, then, to date is that I am deaf in the left ear, bald, subject to mysterious giddy fits and practically cock-eyed . . . My doctor, summing up the subject of my giddy fits and, confessing his inability to explain them, said, 'Well, if you have any more, you'd better just *have* them.' I said I would.
>
> (Letter to William Townend, 14 March 1951)

And so he did – making fun of his various aches and pains to the Constant Readers of his regular correspondence . . . 'It affects me as if I were tight, causing me to lose control of my legs. I'm all right when I'm sitting down but can't navigate' . . . (To Guy Bolton, April 1959). 'What a nuisance it is being 92 and gradually decaying,' he wrote to Ira Gershwin at Christmas 1973. At the time Gershwin himself was a spring chicken of seventy-seven . . .

* * * *

The years passed peacefully enough . . . novel succeeding novel . . . tending to the menagerie that soon contained dogs (plural) *and* cats (ditto) . . . regular walks with friend and neighbour Bolton . . . and the increasingly vocal affection of his public.

Media coverage of his eightieth birthday was remarkable for a man who had hardly been seen in public for a decade:

> I seem to have become the Grand Old Man of English Literature. Grimsdick [his British publisher] tells me they have already received more than five hundred inches of press notices of my birthday and more coming in all the time.
>
> (Letter to Guy Bolton, 28 October 1961)

> Having my octogenarianism hurled at me . . . shook me a bit. I consoled myself with the thought that I can still touch my toes fifty times every morning without a suspicion of bending knees, which I'll bet not many octogenarians can.
>
> (Letter to Denis Mackail, 7 January 1960)

Asked in his mid-eighties if he was afraid of death, he replied – 'Heavens, no. I am far too well balanced. The only thing I ever fear is that the last chapters of any book I write won't work out.'

The octogenarian duly became a nonogenarian and with the same sort of inevitability – a biographer arrived, managed to evade the Cerberus called Ethel, and gave Wodehouse's public its first detailed account of this remarkable life. Anyone who has written about him since owes a debt to David A. Jasen and his *Portrait of a Master*.

There was, of course, the typical Wodehouse smokescreen:

I always thought I was about the dullest subject there was; but he drinks in my every word, blast him. I can't imagine what he thinks he's going to do with the book if he ever writes it. Publishers may be asses, but surely they aren't asses enough to spend money on a thing like that.

Well, fortunately they were and they did.

* * * *

Sir Pelham Grenville Wodehouse – he had been knighted in the 1975 Honours List – died in the local hospital on St Valentine's Day at the age of ninety-three. He had been an American citizen for nearly twenty years by then and his adopted country had made him feel welcome and at home. ('Thank God for being an American,' he wrote to Townend describing his naturalisation, 'And I don't mean God is, I mean I am.') Even so it would not be fanciful to think that a lot of his heart always remained in the land of his birth and the timeless world of which he wrote.

There was occasional talk of a return visit to England but it never came to pass.

I never have any urge to re-visit England, but I do sometimes pine for Scotland. I spent a wonderful week there with Ian Hay a great many years ago, driving from spot to spot playing golf. It's a fascinating country and I don't wonder you have gone back there to live. I feel that I should find England so changed. Everyone tells me I wouldn't recognise London if I saw it again. Not that I did like London much. Nor New York. Edinburgh and Paris are the only two cities.

(Letter to Compton Mackenzie, 10 March 1962)

There were the dogs and so forth to worry about . . . perhaps next year. Besides, it was all a bit of a fag. And then, when the knighthood finally arrived, the years were just too many.

In a 1925 story about Bertie's enforced escape to the USA to avoid an aunt's ire, he had written prophetically:

What I mean is . . . much as I like America I don't want to have England barred to me for the rest of my natural.

The door, in fact, had been ajar for quite a while but, for his own reasons, Wodehouse had never quite chosen to push it open . . .

The unfinished and untitled novel he left by his bedside was fittingly given the posthumous title *Sunset at Blandings*.

Everyone who has read and enjoyed the World According to Wodehouse will have their personal summation of the man and what he stood for but few would disagree with the verdict of his first official biographer, Frances Donaldson, when she wrote: 'He gave happiness to others as few people are privileged to do, and he was happy himself.'

* * * *

At the end of 'The Red-Headed League' Holmes remarks to Watson — '*L'homme c'est rien — l'oeuvre c'est tout,* as Gustave Flaubert wrote to George Sand.'

Wodehouse would almost certainly have agreed. But for once he would not have found *le mot juste* . . . In his case *l'homme* was most certainly not *rien* . . .